STEPHEN E. ROULAC

Welcome to *421 Business Strategy Mistakes and How You Can Avoid Them.* My purpose in writing this book is to enable you to achieve better outcomes in your business involvements.

As important as knowing *what* to do and *how* to do it, knowing what mistakes to avoid can be the difference between whether you get a successful outcome—or you fall short of your objectives. Because strategy is multi-faceted, involving so many choices and interactions, knowing some of the mistakes that could be made can help you avoid them.

This book tells you what you need to know to make superior strategy decisions and have much more enjoyable and rewarding business involvements. May you find this book not only an informative, interesting, and enjoyable reading experience, but also a valuable resource and guide.

Stephen E. Roulac
January 2004

Praise for *421 Business Strategy Mistakes*

"A trove of strategic insights that reads like the *Tao Te Ching* of business. These nuggets of Stephen's good wisdom offer enduring truths with a poetic simplicity that has profound implications. Read this book to absorb strategic understanding at a deep level of consciousness."

—William E. Halal, Professor of Management, George Washington University; Author, *The Infinite Resource* and *Twenty-first Century Economics*

"This is an extraordinary book that will save or make you a fortune. It shows you how to take complete control of your business and financial future."

—Brian Tracy, author, *TurboStrategy*

"Throughout history, it has always been the major battles that have taught us our greatest lessons. People have died trying to discover these truths. This book is like having the golden truths of 421 major battles distilled into their naked essence and handed to you on a silver platter. Just imagine how history would have changed if they had the benefit of this information."
—Thomas J. Frey, Executive Director, The DaVinci Institute

"The concepts in *421 Strategy Mistakes—and How You Can Avoid Them* will win wars, build profitable businesses, and make your life easier and more successful. Knowing what NOT to do will save you a lot of wasted time and energy." —Pam Lontos, PR/PR

"Stephen and I worked closely together for over five years when he was the real estate consultant to CALPERS and I was a manager in the real estate department. We developed a considerable amount of real estate policies after defining our real estate strategy. I was a strong believer in having written policy to guide our decision making policy, and hopefully to avoid some costly mistakes."

—Roger Franz, Former Principal Real Estate Investment Officer, CALPERS

Praise for *421 Business Strategy Mistakes*

"This book summarizes and organizes much of what you learned in business school, and a lot more that your profs may not have taught you. But if you don't want to spend two years and $150,000 in obtaining an MBA, read Steve Roulac's book, which is an outstanding surrogate."
— John W. Bickel II, Co-Founding and Co-Managing Partner, Bickel & Brewer

"Only Stephen Roulac could find 421 ways to make me wince! I suspect every reader will find he or she has been guilty of 200 or more of these mistakes! They serve as critical reminders—one for each day of the year, and a few extras for days you are feeling you really are infallible!"
—Kirk O. Hanson, Professor and Executive Director, Markkula Center for Applied Ethics, Santa Clara University

"The irrefutable lesson of history is that you must avoid mistakes to survive and thrive in turbulent times. Yet even in today's dynamic, highly competitive markets, leaders and managers continue to make mistakes. Businesses and careers are at risk because mistakes are still all too pervasive. Now, finally, there is a book that teaches what you need to know to avoid mistakes. Read and absorb this book to advance your business and career. The alternatives are no longer acceptable."
—Roger Herman, Certified Management Consultant and Strategic Futurist

"This handy and challenging improvement reference—based on stark reality—for the thoughtful business person and student intent on creating success and value is a multi-faceted mirror which reflects, in unforgiving clarity, the wide range of mistakes routinely made by business people everywhere. I found your find book refreshingly direct and to the point."
—Erich A. Helfert, Ph.D., Chairman, Modernsoft, Inc.; Managing Principal, Helfert Associates; author of *Techniques of Financial Analysis,* 11th ed.

Praise for *421 Business Strategy Mistakes*

"This book needed to be written, and Stephen Roulac is the perfect person to do it. No one matches Stephen Roulac's business experience, academic background and strategic insight. *421 Strategy Mistakes and How You Can Avoid Them* is an indispensable checklist for what to look out for in business. This is a great contribution. It is so obvious that it is amazing that it wasn't done a long time ago."
— Loren Volk, CEO, Reality Logic

"Stephen Roulac is a g__d_____ wealth-making genius! In fact, he's one of the three smartest business gurus on the planet! And unlike most geniuses—Stephen has the unique ability to make his brilliant ideas simple to understand and easy to implement... That's rare... His new book, *421 Strategy Mistakes and How You Can Avoid Them*—For Massive Profits!!* R-O-C-K-S! This is brilliant stuff! In fact, it's our business bible that is already putting more millions in our coffers! Now get this: any businessperson who does NOT study and use these 421 strategies is a complete moron that will be crushed in the marketplace by those of us who do know these amazing secrets! (* my addition to the already great title!)."
—T.J. Rohleder, Fonder of M.O.R.E. Incorporated, and author of *Ruthless Marketing*

"If I'd read *421 Strategy Mistakes and How You Can Avoid Them* when I was young and impressionable, I'd probably have won the Republican Senate race for California in '86! Who knows!? It's a must read for anyone who wants to learn what not to do and how to avoid the pitfalls."
—Arthur B. Laffer, Laffer Associates

"I would suggest that the most important strategic mistake anyone might make is missing: 'Failure to purchase this book and review it periodically to avoid all the other possible mistakes!'"
—Norm Matson, Matson Associates

421 Business Strategy Mistakes and How You Can Avoid Them

421 Business Strategy Mistakes

AND HOW YOU CAN AVOID THEM

Stephen E. Roulac

PROPERTY PRESS
San Francisco

ISBN: 1-931578-09-5

Library of Congress Control Number available.

Property Press
709 Fifth Avenue
San Rafael, California 94901

Printed in China by
Palace Press International
San Francisco, California

Dedicated to my son, Arthur Young Roulac, who manifests strategic acumen in action

Contents

Mission

Vision

Decisions

Operating Philosophies

Finance and Accounting

Purchasing and Supply Chain

Styles and Priorities

Management Behavior

Individual Style

Competition and Markets

Perspective and Viewpoints

Marketing and Sales

Organization

Leadership

How You Can Avoid Mistakes

Introduction

In Lewis Carroll's classic book, *Through the Looking Glass*, the Red Queen prophetically informs Alice, "You must run as fast as you can just to stay in the same place. If you want to get ahead, you must run at least twice as fast." Today, however, even running as fast as you can will not necessarily allow you to stay in the same place. To cope with and prevail in the challenges of life today, you need an effective strategy. You need either to do what you did before—very, very well—or to do something differently.

The concept of strategy has its roots in the military-diplomatic strategies of earlier eras, when leaders sought to establish and maintain dominance over a region. Most early writing on strategy is about crafting and executing military strategies.

Strategy today, however, has evolved to mean much more than military strategy. To the person on the street, strategy may mean ways to succeed: tips, tricks and techniques for getting ahead, formulas and shortcuts, good ideas, common sense, the application of logic, or doing whatever people who are successful actually do. In this sense, strategy can be viewed as applied best practice, involving what is described in the Harvard Business School curriculum as "currently useful generalizations."

Everyone has strategies. People have strategies for their different roles in life. In fact, if you think about it, you'll recognize that even your pet, if you have one, has strategies. A pet has strategies to do certain things to get what it wants—be it food, attention, interaction, or a walk.

Just as individuals have strategies, so also do companies. The WalMart strategy has been described as, very simply, a great choice of merchandise and low prices. The Tiffany strategy, by contrast, is the highest quality merchandise and the best designs. WalMart does not expect to provide its customers much service, whereas Tiffany provides considerable service. Each has a distinctive and very different strategy. Each strategy is successful.

Strategy can mean different things to different people. Some think strategy refers to only the highest level decisions, concerning *which, when* and *what.* For others, strategy is much more about *how to.* Some differentiate strategy from tactics, with tactics being shorter-term, smaller-scale actions, while strategy is concerned with the longer term and the larger scale. Some of the mistakes in *421 Strategy Mistakes and How You Can Avoid Them* could be considered tactics by some.

No matter what strategy means to you, or how others define strategy, a universal truth—unarguable and indisputable—is that every individual and every organization—be it a business or government agency or non-governmental organization—at some time or another, makes strategy mistakes. Not all companies achieve the leadership that WalMart and Tiffany have. Many companies make mistakes in choosing and implementing their strategies.

In any important sporting event, the outcome is more often determined by mistakes than brilliant plays. The team that makes the fewest mistakes often wins the game. Similarly, the company that makes the fewest mistakes often achieves higher profits than companies that makes many mistakes. Strategy mistakes can be the difference between success and failure. Strategy mistakes can take what could otherwise be a marvelous outcome and cause it to be unrewarding, disappointing or even a major failure.

421 Strategy Mistakes and How You Can Avoid Them is intended to help you learn from those who have already made mistakes, so that you do not have to learn by repeating those same mistakes. Those who have less background in strategy will encounter insights, perspectives and strategies that would take much study and decades of experience to gain. Some strategists will likely find this book to be a useful refresher of proven success strategies.

Given the breadth and scope of the strategy discipline, the mistakes selected for inclusion should be thought of as a representative rather than comprehensive collection—a sampling rather than a complete full-course meal. Many of the mistakes that apply to organizational behavior are directly applicable to individual behavior, and vice versa. For some readers, many of the mistakes listed here will be familiar. You may find yourself nodding in recognition, remembering the time you saw very similar mistakes being committed. Hopefully, they did not cost you, your company, or your investments too much money.

The style of presentation in this book is succinct and to the point. By way of gender terminology, he and she are interchangeable, and there is no presumption that men or women are more or less inclined to make any one mistake. Although the presentation that follows is organized into general categories, there is no particular ordering of mistakes within these categories. Rather, the presentation is designed to accommodate whatever sequence or even random order that the reader may choose.

421 Strategy Mistakes and How You Can Avoid Them aims to help you achieve your business, investing, and personal objectives. Avoiding the strategy mistakes that follow by no means guarantees that you will have outstanding outcomes or results. But if you avoid at least the majority of the mistakes that follow, you'll have a much better chance of achieving outstanding results than if you fall prey to some or many of these mistakes.

PLANS AND GOALS

1 No Plan

A surprising number of companies operate with no plan.

If you operate with no plan, you are proceeding in reliance on spontaneous, reactive, and even impromptu action—rather than on the basis of deliberate, considered approaches to the business. If what is to be done is not much thought about in advance, the opportunity for reflection, consideration and choosing the best way is quite limited. Without a plan, the benefits of plans—focus on priorities, assignment of responsibilities, accountability for results—cannot be realized. Enterprises with plans achieve greater and more frequent success than those that lack them. For as it has insightfully been said, failing to plan is planning to fail.

Not having a plan is a mistake.

2 No Written Plan

Some companies actually have plans, but the plans are never written down.

A written plan is far superior to an unwritten plan. It has been said that until a plan is written down, it does not exist. The process of writing imposes a certain discipline and forces consideration of issues and their implications for the business. A written plan can facilitate communication to and by others. A plan that is written is more likely to be realized than a plan that is not.

Failing to express a plan in writing is a mistake.

3 Plans for Show, Not for Go

Some companies have plans that are designed more to be shown to others than to be implemented.

Companies may put together a "business plan" whose primary purpose is to raise money rather than to guide operations. Preparing even a sham business plan—if it involves at least a little genuine thinking through of priorities and tasks, consideration of how different business issues are interrelated, and writing it all down—is certainly better than not having thought about these things at all. But a plan that is prepared but not applied is much less relevant, useful and valuable than one that is actually embraced, applied and implemented.

Plans that are for show and not for go are a mistake.

4 Plans for the Shelf, Not for Action

Some companies have a major commitment to preparing plans, but much less of a commitment to following plans.

Some companies will regularly go through a serious planning process, with the results organized, compiled, and presented in a fancy binder. The problem is that the fancy binder is put on the shelf—but not implemented. The plan stays on the shelf until it is consulted for the next planning process. While companies that engage in preparing plans for the shelf are better off than companies that engage in no planning at all, plans that sit on the shelf are much less useful than plans that are implemented.

Preparing plans for the shelf rather than for implementation is a mistake.

5 Confusing Plans and Strategies

Plans and strategies are interrelated, but not the same thing.

The term *strategic planning* causes many to think that plans and strategy mean the same thing—or that if you address *plans* you have addressed *strategy*. Not so. Strategy theorist Henry Mintzberg points out that strategy is about *ends* and *distinction*, while planning is about the *means* and *process*.

Businesses need both strategies and plans. Strategies represent a higher level of thinking in relation to what the business is about and how it is going to get there. Planning is concerned with how strategies will be implemented. Strategy should come first, followed by the plan of how to implement the strategy. The output of the planning process is the plan that serves as the roadmap to guide implementation.

Confusing plans with strategies and planning with strategizing is a mistake.

6 Plans Without a Strategy

Some companies have plans, but they have no strategy.

A plan without a strategy reflects a narrow, limited, lower level view of a business. If you have a plan without a strategy, you may get done what you set out to do, but it may not be the right thing. The strategy represents the conceptual connection of the enterprise's mission, values and goals. The plan provides a more detailed road map of how to get from point A to point B.

A plan without a strategy is a mistake.

7 Lack of Policies

The difference between a successful and unsuccessful business enterprise is often attributable to the commitment to, implementation of and consistent application of the policies that guide the enterprise's decisions.

Research into what contributes most to superior stock performance has conclusively shown that policy decisions have a much greater impact on investment performance than does the analysis of a specific stock. Similarly, in a business setting the policy decisions that guide the enterprise's direction and priorities exert much more impact upon ultimate business performance than does a single transaction. In practice, all too many enterprises operate without policies, or if they have policies, the policies are too often inappropriate or incomplete or inadequately articulated.

Lack of effective policies is a mistake.

8 Making Decisions in a Policy Vacuum

Some companies approach decision making without considering the policy implications of those decisions.

Decisions made in a policy vacuum can be bad decisions. If you do not consider the consequences of decisions upon larger concerns and priorities, you may make a very different decision than you would had you considered such consequences. Recognizing the importance of policies to guide decisions, institutional investors manage their portfolios in the context of particular investment policies. Without an appropriate investment policy, it is all too easy to end up in a situation—as has happened with more than a few portfolios—where a collection of individual decisions resulted in a basket of investments that collectively reflected a much worse outcome than had an investment policy been adhered to. In this case the whole was much worse than the sum of the parts.

Failing to consider the policy implications of decisions is a mistake.

9 Designing New Policy to Solve Yesterday's Problem

There is a saying that it doesn't do much good to close the barn door after the horses have run away. The same thing applies in business strategy.

All too often, companies put in place policies that are intended to solve yesterday's problem. The high-profile issue commands attention. People insist something be done. So management puts in place a policy that is intended to address that issue. The trouble with this approach is that the next problem is unlikely to be the same as the last problem. The company should be thinking ahead to design and implement policies for the future, not the past.

It is a mistake to put in place a policy to address yesterday's problem.

10 Inconsistency in Corporate Policy

Companies that do not maintain consistent policies do so at their peril.

In one instance, a company insisted that it could not track critical cost information to provide what a certain customer wished to know. Yet that same company, in another customer relationship, had committed to and was in fact tracking the same critical cost information. Understandably, the first customer was unhappy when it found out that the company was in fact contractually committed to do, and was actually doing, what it claimed it could not do.

To represent that you cannot do for one customer what you in fact are doing for another is a mistake.

11 Lack of a Specific Business Goal

If you are going to be in business, you had better be clear about your destination.

If you proceed in any direction without a specific business goal, you may get to just any destination. The destination you get to may or may not be the destination you really want. Lacking clarity as to your end destination, you have no way of making the myriad decisions you will encounter along the way.

To lack a clear idea of your end destination can be a mistake.

12 Unmeasurable Business Goals

As important as goals are, if they cannot be measured, it is difficult to know whether you have achieved the desired outcome.

Business goals that can be measured are much more powerful than those that cannot. Fortunately, virtually every goal can be measured. Even qualitative considerations, such as “customer satisfaction” or “leading supplier in XYZ market” or “most respected company,” are susceptible to measurement. Lacking measurable business goals, the prospects of achieving the desired outcome are compromised.

To fail to establish measurable business goals can be a mistake.

STRATEGY

13 Strategic Incongruency

Strategy, to be effective, must be congruent.

If balance and consistency between different parts of the business strategy are lacking, the resulting incongruence compromises the prospects of business success. Strategy congruency means that there is a reasonable connection between one part of a strategy and another part of a strategy. The purposes of one part of the enterprise are complementary to those of another part of the enterprise. The goals of one division are supportive of, and in parallel with, the goals of another division.

Some time ago a prominent investment firm, known for its highly disciplined quantitative corporate securities investment management style, elected to diversify its product offerings to a non-traditional investment area. The idea of expanding the menu of investment products to its clients was sound, but the way the investment firm went about doing it was wholly incongruent with its basic business strategy. While the executives in the established investment business were highly disciplined in how they made investment decisions, the executives in the non-traditional field were highly informal, implicit, and unstructured in how they made investment decisions. Investors accustomed to one style in the primary business encountered a very different style in the new business. The lack of strategic congruency was a major reason for the disappointing performance of the new venture, which in turn compromised the success of the primary business.

A lack of strategy congruency is a mistake.

14 Too Much Strategy Input

While it is important to get access to multiple sources of input when making important strategy decisions, sometimes too much input can be as bad or worse than too little.

If managers spend too many resources on considering what to do, to the point that action is too protracted and delayed—or never happens at all—it could be worse than not getting any input. A manager must balance the importance of input, specifically getting enough to have breadth of prospective, but not spending so much time in getting input that the quality of the decision is compromised.

Getting too much input for important strategy decisions can be a mistake.

15 Combining Strategy and Communications

The strategy and communication roles involve very different functions and purposes.

Strategy is concerned with deciding what to do. Then, once a strategy decision has been made, communication is concerned with telling those who need to know what is to be done. Though strategy decisions should include consideration of communication concerns, if disproportionate emphasis is placed on message delivery at the expense of message content, deficient decisions can result.

One of the lead advisors to United Kingdom Prime Minister Tony Blair held the title of Director of Strategy and Communications. Certainly, combining these two functions facilitates integration of the dual perspectives—but does it necessarily promote the best strategy decisions? Might spin and public image considerations undesirably color the decision process? Combining in one role jobs with different and sometimes conflicting functions can be an invitation to deficient decision making.

Inappropriately combining strategy and communication roles is a mistake.

16 Failing to Review Contracts To Consider Impacts on New Strategy Directions

Companies often pursue new strategies and directions with the objective of challenging the past.

A new strategy direction intended to challenge the past must, by definition, raise issues that will be of concern to those who have major investments in the past. Much of the literature concerning change is about the consequences of change for organization practices and people's patterns of doing things. Too little considered are the implications of a new strategy direction on existing contractual commitments.

At the time a company plans a new strategy direction, it is crucial to review contractual commitments, in order to determine the compatibility of those contractual commitments to that strategy direction. If there is incompatibility, the issues should be addressed immediately, not put off until the middle of a major transaction or, as sometimes can be the case, after the fact. Raising contractual issues under the pressure of making a deal, or after the fact when a violation has already occurred, can be a very expensive proposition.

Failing to review contracts to consider impacts of new strategy directions can be a mistake.

VALUES

17 Values Lacking in Commitment

Some companies develop a statement of values because the management textbooks say that companies should have a values statement.

But a values statement that is prepared for appearance rather than substance is not especially valuable. Values that reflect articulation of a commitment to higher purposes are much more impactful than those that reflect a *going-through-the-motions* approach. Empty values are not nearly as valuable as values that are anchored in commitments.

A values statement for appearance's sake rather than to reflect commitments is a mistake.

18 Decisions Independent of Values

If decisions are made independently of values, those decisions are less likely to be the right ones for a company than if the company's values are specifically considered in the decision process.

Values can provide guidance to company employees by enabling them to make decisions that are consistent with what the company stands for and what the company aspires to be. While many people can readily make decisions when confronted with a familiar situation, relying on what has been done before, an unfamiliar situation can be more challenging. Values can provide the means for employees to make decisions in an unfamiliar situation and in circumstances that they have not encountered before. Referencing company values to guide unfamiliar decisions, especially when there is no logical precedent, can meaningfully increase the likelihood that decisions made are the right ones for the company.

Making decisions without considering company values is a mistake.

19 Responding to Decisions Without a Value Anchor

The decision style employed can have an important influence on the ability of a manager to achieve desired strategic outcomes.

Some executives make decisions without a uniform, consistent theme between one decision and another. Other managers make decisions from a core of specified values that provide a reference point to determine what is the best decision, not merely for short-term benefit, but over the long haul.

To make decisions without a firmly articulated set of values can be a mistake.

MISSION

20 No Mission Statement

Too many companies operate without a mission statement.

A mission statement provides guidance to those who are taking the company's message to the market. The mission statement reflects a company's purposes, what it is about, and what it is seeking to do. To comprehend the consequences of no mission statement, think about what might happen if missionaries were sent out into the field to spread the word, but they did not know what word they were to spread.

The absence of a mission statement is a mistake.

21 Mission Confusion

An organization's mission should reflect clarity rather than confusion.

A mission statement that reflects confused thinking can compromise the organization's realization of its objectives. If you send people on a mission, you want them to be absolutely clear about what their mission is. You do not want some people pursuing one thing and some pursuing another thing.

Confusion concerning the company's mission statement is a mistake.

22 Unrecognized Shifting Mission

A company's mission may, over time, evolve into something new.

Unless a company consciously makes a decision to change its mission, the company's mission is expected to represent stability, consistency and continuity. But if the mission creeps from one thing to another thing, perhaps without the organization being aware of what is really happening, the organization may find that its mission has evolved to be something other than what was anticipated—or even desired. The shift in mission may result in a mission that is less relevant or less useful than was originally intended. While it might be perfectly all right and sometimes good for a mission to evolve, the company should recognize such an evolution of its mission, and should re-write and re-clarify its mission statement.

Allowing a mission to unconsciously shift over time can be a mistake.

23 Can't Answer "What Business are You In?" Question

If a company does not have a good answer to the question, "What business are you in?" then that company does not really have its act together.

If all the people in the company cannot effectively tell someone what business the company is in, then how will they know how to make effective decisions? How will those employees be able to recognize opportunities? How will those employees be able to respond to customer inquiries?

Inability to answer the "What business are you in?" question is a mistake.

VISION

24 Lack of Vision

Some enterprises operate without a vision.

Lack of vision may reflect a nose-to-the-grindstone approach to business. The involvement in the here and now is so intense, so all-consuming, that larger possibilities are given little thought. The company figuratively keeps putting one step in front of another, without consideration of what might be possible or desirable. Without a vision, what might be accomplished with a vision is unlikely to be accomplished.

Lack of a vision is mistake.

25 Limited Vision

Some companies develop visions that are limited.

A limited vision is often the result of limitations imposed by the company's present resources and circumstances, or by the company's limited view of what is possible. The primary purpose of a vision is to consider what could be, if current constraints, perceptions, circumstances and resources were relaxed or even removed. An expansive vision can, in itself, provide the inspiration and ultimately the means towards realization. But if the vision is limited, the prospects of achieving a grander vision will be neither considered nor realized.

A limited vision is a limiting vision, and is a mistake.

26 Trophy Vision

Some companies, knowing that vision is what they are expected to have, develop a trophy vision.

A trophy vision serves the objective of impressing others rather than motivating those within the company. Trophy vision is designed more for "show" than for "go." A vision should reflect resonance with the people who are going to pursue it—not be designed to impress others. Although a company's vision may, in fact, be impressive to others, that outcome should be a byproduct of the vision that serves the company's aspirations, and not the primary emphasis of the vision.

A trophy vision, intended to impress others rather than to serve the company, may be a mistake.

27 Searching for New Vision When It Is Not Really Needed

In recent years, the importance of *vision* has been straongly emphasized.

Often, when a new leader assumes the chief executive officer position, that individual may advocate the need for a new vision. But sometimes, a new vision may be inappropriate, distracting, or worse. When Lou Gerstner became CEO of IBM, he proclaimed that the last thing that IBM needed was a new vision. Rather, he asserted, IBM should concentrate on doing its basic business.

To emphasize a new vision when that is not what is really needed can be a mistake.

28 Championing Vision at the Expense of Validation

In recent years, business publications and management journals have been fixated on *vision.*

As important as vision is to a company, if there is no validity behind the vision, all may be for naught. Validity behind the vision takes care to ensure that there is credibility, reality, and reliability—along with the high-sounding vision. To succeed, you need vision *and* validation, high-octane ideas *and* high-level performance, motivating aspirations *and* pragmatic substance.

To champion vision but forget about validation is a mistake.

29 Not Knowing Where You Are Going

There is a saying that if you do not know where you are going, any road will take you there.

Many companies are apparently just meandering along "any road." One might conclude that many companies do not know where they are going. When a company is not very explicit and directed in the path it is pursuing, it is quite possible the company is not very clear about its ultimate destination.

Not knowing where you are going can be a mistake.

DECISIONS

30 Indecisiveness

All too many companies are plagued by indecisiveness.

Indecisiveness actually reflects the decision not to make a decision. Not making a decision means embracing the status quo and rejecting the choices of what could be available, were a decision to be made. The advantages of making a decision, even if it is the wrong decision, is that one can gain feedback from the consequences of the decision and make adjustments as appropriate. But if you never make a decision you never have a chance to see what might happen and to incorporate that information into a future choice.

Indecisiveness is a mistake.

31 Shoot-from-the-Hip Decisions

Some companies employ a shoot-from-the-hip decision style.

The gunslinger of the old Wild West had to draw quickly and shoot quickly, from the hip, in response to whatever danger might come his way. Of course, certain of the legendary gunslingers were extremely strategic and calculating in how they set up their confrontations, manipulating circumstances to their maximum advantage. Others, who tended to have very short careers as gunslingers, were less anticipatory, less strategic in how they approached their confrontations, with the consequence that they had relatively few confrontations to worry about, for in a short period of time they came out on the wrong side of the shootout. By incorporating strategy, preparation and calculations into decisions, better decisions can be made.

Shoot-from-the-hip decisions can be a mistake.

32 Too-Late Decisions

Making decisions too late can have very dire consequences.

The aphorism about shutting the barn door after the horse is already out of the barn is applicable in many managerial settings. A decision properly made anticipates when the decision is needed, and then executes that decision on a timely basis. When a decision is made too late, the benefits that might have been achieved by a timely decision are lost.

Making a decision too late is a mistake.

33 Too-Soon Decisions

Just as it is inappropriate to make a decision too late, it can be inappropriate to make a decision too soon.

If a decision is made too soon, information that might later become available is not considered. A decision made too soon may motivate some people to be less focused and less concentrated than they might be, were the decision resolution still uncertain. While in some instances certainty can be a positive, in others, it can be a negative, as the benefits of uncertainty are inevitably sacrificed.

Making decisions too soon is a mistake.

34 Ignoring Strategic Significance of Key Provisions of Contract

Although contracts necessarily and appropriately are the domain of legal counsel, contracts also have strategic significance.

To ignore the strategic implications of a contract—what its provisions make possible or constrain—can be a major mistake. A contract needs to be evaluated not just in terms of legal criteria, but also, and especially, in terms of strategic criteria. Contracts effectively specify what the company can do and what it cannot do.

To ignore the strategic significance of key provisions of a contract is a mistake.

35 Failing to Have the Right Business Model

If the company does not have the right business model, its prospects for success are meaningfully compromised.

The company's business model can be thought of as a collection of the "hows"—of how the company does business, how it interacts with customers, how it produces the goods and services it sells, and how it organizes and coordinates the relationships among the different stakeholders. Having the right business model is fundamental to business success. If you have the right business model, you have a good chance to be successful. If you have the wrong business model, success is a long-odds proposition.

It is a mistake to have the wrong business model.

36 Fixed Rigid Business Model

Every business operates with a business model. If the business model is right for the times, the company may achieve great success. If it is not, the company will not.

As important as it is to get the business model right, it is also important to realize that the business model should be dynamic. To the extent the company's resources change, a new business model may be appropriate. To the extent that competitors implement new ways of doing business, a new business model may be appropriate. To the extent that customers have changing expectations and resources, a new business model may be needed.

To stick unvaryingly to the same business model can be a mistake.

37 Refusing to Reassess the Business Model

If you have the right business model over time, your odds of success are much greater than if you do not.

Up until the time of the personal computer revolution, IBM dominated the information technology business because of its insistence on a proprietary environment for its computer systems. Once you bought into the IBM product line, you had few options to do business with anyone else. The decision to go with IBM also meant you had essentially agreed to be subjected to IBM's virtual monopoly on your future options. But when the personal computer innovation revolutionized information technology, insistence on the proprietary system became a liability. By aggressively moving away from that business model and embracing an open architecture standard technologies approach, IBM reemerged as a dominant technology player.

To refuse to revise your business model can be a mistake.

38 No Contingency Plan

Astute companies operate with contingency plans.

A contingency plan anticipates what could go wrong and provides for appropriate responses to what can go wrong. Effective contingency planning follows from the maxim to expect the best, but plan for the worst. If you do not have a contingency plan when something goes wrong, you may not be in a position to respond. Without a contingency plan, you could be stuck in a very awkward, inappropriate, expensive and embarrassing place.

Not having a contingency plan is a mistake.

39 No Answer to "What's Next?" Question

Fundamental in business is thinking about how to answer the question "What's next?"

The "What's next?" question is important in many ways. Customers want to know what you're going to do for them next. If you don't think about what you're going to do for the customers next, you will not be well positioned to provide an effective, responsive, helpful answer to the customer's "What's next?" question. You will not meet the customer's needs. Even if you come up with some off-the-cuff, impromptu answer, you will not be in a position to deliver effectively on that answer, because you have not thought through sufficiently what you need to do to have an effective response to the "What's next?" question.

Unless you prepare to have a good answer to the "What's next?" question, you are making a mistake.

OPERATING PHILOSOPHIES

40 Failing to Employ a Structured Decision Process

Decisions made without a structured, systematic process may be less than optimal.

Business school courses, academic textbooks, and training programs concerning decision making provide structured approaches, decision models, and tips to make better decisions. The classic approach involves defining the problem, identifying alternatives, undertaking quantitative analyses and qualitative assessments, exploring the risks, and then choosing the best course of action. While a structured decision making process is central to management, too often that approach is ignored.

Failing to employ a structured decision process can be a mistake.

41 Not Understanding the Costs of Implementing a Structured Decision Process

Decisions have costs.

While a structured decision making process can result in a better decision and a more cost-effective and proper use of resources, you must also consider that decision making is not free. There is cost involved in implementing the decision process itself.

If you do not understand the costs of implementing structured decision making processes, you may make a mistake.

42 Disregarding Costs of Deciding on a Managerial Methodology

Business schools, management treatises and training workshops are devoted to teaching managerial methods and decision making.

Despite all of the resources and attention devoted to teaching managerial methods, seldom is the question of the cost of implementing a management method addressed. Most approaches to management practice seem to presume that there is no cost of implementing a particular method.

Some of the costs involved in implementing management methodologies are:

- acquiring valuable software tools;
- supplying training and continuing education to use software and management tools;
- accessing, developing, and procuring information to be utilized in the analysis of which methodology is needed;
- time spent in evaluating the results of the analysis to make the decision; and
- time spent in implementing the methodology.

If you fail to consider the costs of applying different management methods, you may miscalculate, by adopting business approaches that have much greater costs than realistically recognized.

Failing to recognize the costs of employing management methods can be a mistake.

43 Unwillingness to Shift Priorities

A basic Business 101 lesson is to establish priorities and stick to them.

Students of business are taught the importance of establishing priorities and sticking to them. By determining what is most important and then doing it, superior outcomes can be achieved. However, as important as establishing and following through on priorities is, it is a mistake to resist shifting priorities when evidence of different conditions and new opportunities suggest it would be advisable to do so. Markets change, established approaches are threatened and new opportunities emerge, with the result that sticking to initial priorities can result in disappointment, if not worse.

To stick to priorities when evidence suggests it would be better to alter them can be a strategic mistake.

44 Persist in Doing What You've Always Done

There is a saying that if you always do what you've always done, you will always get what you have always gotten.

So long as you keep doing what you have always done, you will likely get the same outcomes. If those outcomes are exactly what you want—fine. But if those outcomes are in any way short of what you want, then you need to reassess whether improved outcomes would be brought about by continuing to do what you've always done—or whether improved outcomes might more likely be achieved by doing something different. By doing different things and things differently, you can meaningfully improve the results you might achieve than if you just do more of the same.

To keep doing what you've always been doing rather than doing something new can be a mistake.

45 Lack of Executive Support for New Initiatives

When a company embarks on a new initiative, support of senior executives is critical.

Studies of what makes for successful change programs are virtually unanimous in identifying the most important factor as the commitment and support of the chief executive. If senior executives' support is lacking, the prospects of the new initiative being successfully implemented are remote. Without senior executive support, the prospects of achieving success are much diminished.

To embark upon a new initiative without senior executive support is a mistake.

46 Failing to Confirm the Integrity of the Underlying Core Competence

Sometimes, the excitement and appeal of heading off in a new business direction can cause leaders to lose sight of the fundamental importance of the company's core competence.

If the company does not possess fundamental integrity and vitality in its most basic capabilities—if its core competence is somehow flawed—then the company's capacity to achieve its objectives is inherently comprised. No amount of emphasis on new business directions can make up for defects in the company's core competence.

Emphasizing other priorities, when the company's core competence is compromised, can be a mistake.

47 Not Considering How a New Venture May Impact an Existing Commitment

In strategizing a new enterprise commitment, it is important to look not just ahead but also to look back.

Why is it important to look back when strategizing a new commitment? Any new commitment must be built upon not only the foundation of the present, but also and especially the past. Prior decisions, undertakings, and commitments all influence future commitments. To plan a new undertaking without considering how prior commitments may impact that undertaking can result in disappointment, liability and damages.

To plan a new commitment without considering how that new commitment may be impacted by prior commitments can be a mistake.

48 Persisting with a Business Initiative in Light of Contrary Market Feedback

Sometimes, when expected results are not achieved, the conclusion is that more time is needed. The idea is that you can just keep working at it, and eventually results will come. In many circumstances, that can be the outcome, but not always.

If expected results are not achieved, it is important to consider why not. It may be that some modification, adjustment and refinement are called for. Perhaps some slight change can have a dramatic impact upon the desired outcome.

To persist in doing something, without assessment or modification, can be a mistake.

49 Big Picture Blindness: *Bridge Over the River Kwai* Effect

Excellence in performing a given task does not necessarily mean that the task will help achieve a desired outcome or even should be performed at all.

In the Second World War, a group of British soldiers, imprisoned in a Japanese prison camp, were forced to build a bridge over the River Kwai. With admirable and typical *esprit de corps* and a *can-do* attitude, the British prisoners built a magnificent bridge. What they did not appreciate or consider sufficiently was that the bridge they were building was intended to assist their enemy in winning the war. Focusing on the task at hand distracted them from consideration of the larger purpose.

Emphasizing the immediate task at the expense of the larger purpose can be a mistake.

50 Emphasizing Revenues Over Profits

Some companies are committed to maximizing revenues, with the idea that if revenues are high enough, profits inevitably follow. Not necessarily.

The crucial metric is business profit, the difference between revenue and expense. If one consequence of maximizing revenues is to increase expenses dramatically so that profits are diminished, the outcome may be much less satisfactory than a much smaller revenue volume with a much higher profit. The astute strategist focuses on the spread between revenues and expenses, rather than just the overall magnitude of revenue.

Emphasizing revenue at the expense of profit can be a mistake.

51 Promoting Traffic at the Expense of Profitability

Seeking to establish themselves in a new market, some companies may emphasize customer traffic—to the exclusion of whether they make any money on those so-called customers.

As Peter Drucker has observed, it is a fundamental business truth that the purpose of business is to create and retain a customer. But if you do not make any money on your customers, you do not have a business. Generating traffic without revenue and profitable customer transactions is a sure way to financial ruin. This lesson was relearned by many dot-com technology companies in the 1990s, who promoted traffic to their websites but failed to establish a viable business model. Numerous dot-com companies that failed did not sufficiently understand that, at the end of the day, maximizing hits is much less important than generating revenues in amounts more than the expenses incurred in achieving those revenues, so that the business can make a profit and sustain itself.

Promoting customer traffic at the expense of good business is a mistake.

52 Emphasizing Growth at the Expense of Value

Some companies pursue growth strategies irrespective of the economic value associated with those growth strategies.

In stock market investing, a growth strategy is premised upon the idea that profitability will take care of itself. The basic momentum of expanding revenues will somehow lead to profitability and therefore business value. But the emphasis on growth can obscure considerations of value. Renowned investor Warren Buffet cogently observes that growth and value should be thought of together, not as separate and apart. The company's capacity to grow is part of its value. Growth that does not lead to profitability is really of no value.

Pursuing growth without consideration of its value consequences is a mistake.

53 Concentrating on Being the Biggest

Some companies are absorbed with the idea of being the biggest in the business.

Companies that want to be the biggest may emphasize any number of scale metrics—revenues, employees, numbers of outlets, numbers of customers, numbers of products. Although in certain instances having the most of something can be crucial to meeting customer needs, achieving competitive advantage and maximizing profits, by no means is the quest for biggest synonymous with company profitability.

Concentrating too much attention on being the biggest can be a mistake.

54 Thinking Big Size Is Enough

Many think that mere size is sufficient to merit business leadership.

Large organizations have long expected and commanded respect. The thinking goes that if the company attracted that many customers and employees, it must be doing something right. The decisions and actions that enabled the company to grow generated respect, which high regard and respect may continue long beyond what might be justified by an objective assessment of recent actions and outcomes. Even though IBM faltered in the mid-1980s, for many years that company ranked high in the list of the most admired companies. Eventually, the consequences of negative outcomes compounded, causing IBM to fall substantially in stature, although in more recent years it has rebounded. The experience of IBM and many other companies underscores the reality that big scale alone is not enough to achieve business success.

Thinking that size alone is enough to achieve business success is a mistake.

55 Being Too Greedy

In today's highly competitive business climate, leaders and managers of companies are under great pressure to produce strong financial results.

In earlier times investors tended to be satisfied with a company having a good reputation and making good products. Today, investors insist on outstanding financial performance. For many investors, reputation and product quality are important *only* if they lead to superior financial performance in the form of higher profits and higher stock prices. In the search to achieve superior financial performance, some companies may be motivated to pursue profits at any cost. This profiteering objective sometimes overwhelms considerations of common sense, ethics and legality. When companies become too greedy, they can end up doing things that destroy what was otherwise a sound business. The debacles at Enron and Arthur Andersen are only a recent chapter in that story.

Being too greedy can be a mistake.

56 Emphasizing the Wrong Things

In business, you make continual choices about what to focus on. If you emphasize the wrong thing, this can lead to disappointing and even disastrous results.

On his deathbed, Louis XIV issued a prophetic, but ultimately ignored, warning that inappropriate *reliance on dancers and architects* would bring inevitable financial disaster. The parallel business lesson is that disproportionate attention to entertainment and design, as important as these themes are, can be disastrous. Too much frivolity at the expense of serious work is a prescription for disappointment—as is a disproportionate emphasis on aesthetics at the expense of functionality.

Emphasizing the wrong things can be a mistake.

57 Disregarding Significance of Context

Too many emphasize content, without similar consideration to context.

The context in which a decision is to be made is at least as important as the substance or content of that decision. When Jean Claude Gasse was a senior research executive at Apple Computer, he observed that taking context into account was worth at least 50 IQ points. Content without context is susceptible to misinterpretation and miscalculation. If you have an important strategy decision to make, you ignore context at your peril.

Ignoring context is a mistake.

58 Insufficient Attention to Cultural Context

Comprehending cultural context is crucial to business success.

Cultures have their own rules, procedures and favored protocol. The culture exerts a strong influence upon how things are done in that particular organization and place. Culture affects both the legal system and the *ropes to know* and the *ropes to avoid.* To be effective, you need to understand how the culture influences the way business is done in that particular place.

Insufficient attention to culture can be a mistake.

59 Working Harder

Some companies hope to prevail in the market by working harder. The idea is that if you work harder—a putting in more hours, working more intensely, out-hustling the competition—you will get ahead.

In certain circumstances, working harder is the crucial differentiating factor. Legendary Green Bay Packers football coach Vince Lombardi was renowned for the demanding workouts he put his football team through. Every day in his practice sessions he reinforced his maxim, "Anything is possible, if you're willing to pay the price." His teams enjoyed great success, largely attributable to all of the hard work they had done before the game was played.

Everything else being equal, the individual or team that works the hardest will likely prevail over the individual or team that doesn't work so hard. But working harder is not the only important consideration. Working smart, being effective and calculating in what you do and how you do it, is as or more important.

Thinking that the only way to get ahead is to work harder can be a mistake.

60 Exploit the Employee

Some companies operate with an *exploit the employee* approach.

Some companies reason that employees are out to take advantage of them, so the company should get everything it can from the employee. A company may figure that it is paying the employee good money and that therefore nothing more is due or expected. If the employee doesn't like it, the employee can go somewhere else. After all, there are many other people the company could hire. But will an *exploit the employee* approach attract and keep the best employees?

Exploiting the employee can be a mistake.

61 Emphasizing Rules over Creativity

As important as procedures and rules are to business success, if they are disproportionately emphasized over creativity, the business may suffer.

Rules and procedures provide guidance to assure consistent, uniform performance. Rules and procedures that promote consistency can lead to customer satisfaction and loyalty. But rules and procedures, blindly followed, can be dangerous. Often, the right decision requires creativity to do something that had not been previously considered. Creativity can enhance and extend the impact of rules and procedures.

Relying on rules and procedures at the expense of creativity can be a mistake.

62 Exploit the Supplier

Some companies adopt an *exploit the supplier* approach.

The companies that adopt an *exploit the supplier* approach reason that they are paying the supplier good money and therefore should get everything they possibly can out of the supplier. The company may feel that what they don't take from the supplier, the supplier will take from them. So the company approaches its dealings with suppliers from an exploitative, as contrasted to a cooperative approach. But will *exploit the supplier* motivate the best suppliers to want to do business with the company over the long term?

Exploiting the supplier can be a mistake.

63 Exploit the Customer

Some companies and executives operate with an *exploit the customer* approach.

The apparent justification to the *exploit the customer* approach is that it's just a transaction, the customer should look after himself, and if the customer doesn't like it, that is the customer's tough luck. After all, there are many customers and any unhappy current customer can be replaced. Further, the business reasons that its purpose is to get as much advantage, economic gain, and benefit from the customer as possible. But will exploiting the customer build a lasting customer base?

Exploiting the customer can be a mistake.

64 Pollute the Environment

Some companies operate with the idea that they may as well just get rid of their waste by throwing it away and spewing it into the air, water, or ground.

Those companies seem not to care about others. Maybe those companies simply do not think about it. Maybe they justify their behavior by saying everyone does it. Maybe they rationalize what they do by claiming they cannot afford to pay the costs of their own cleanup and waste removal. Separate and apart from the irresponsibility of such conduct, extraordinary legal liability including fines, damages, and criminal charges can result from such conduct.

Polluting the environment can be a very expensive mistake.

65 Emphasizing *Getting it Done* over *Getting it Right*

Some companies are so insistent on *getting it done* that they subordinate any concerns for *getting it right.*

As important as getting it done is, there can be a downside to an excessive *do it now* approach that does not take into consideration the consequences of such an approach. The thinking is that it is better to get it done and then get it right later, than not to get it done. While in some instances this approach may be the best approach, in other instances it is not. You need to be discerning as to when it is appropriate to consider the consequences in advance.

Emphasizing getting it done over getting it right can be a mistake.

66 Too Much in a Hurry to Get it Right

One of the mantras of business today is speed.

Speed in business takes the form of compressed cycle times, fast turnaround, prompt responses to inquiries and short production cycles. Aggressive, result-oriented leaders insist on a do-it-now mentality rather than a do-it-later or do-it-sometime approach. But if you are in too much of a hurry to get it done, if you fail to take the time to think it through carefully, if you fail to get it right, you may find you miscalculate.

Being in too much of a hurry to get it done can be a mistake.

67 Insufficient Consultation before Making Important Decisions

Research has shown that multiple inputs to decisions are often superior to very limited input.

Anyone who has attended an effective case-discussion-based learning environment, such as that employed at Harvard Business School and certain other schools that emphasize the case method, readily recognizes that others can bring a perspective, point of view, or frame of reference to a decision that may be very different from how a single individual might approach that decision. By gaining more points of view, a manager may make superior decisions. If insufficient attention is directed to others' points of view, decisions may be overly narrow.

To make a decision without gaining access to sufficient points of view can be a mistake.

68 Not Retaining an Advisor

Many executives employ a lone wolf, *go-it-alone* style. Rather than retaining a professional advisor, these executives rely on their own insights.

There can be various reasons executives choose not to retain a professional advisor. Working with a professional advisor can take more time than going it alone. The advisor may come up with ideas or issues that slow down the program or involve additional costs to address. The executive may perceive that too much education is required to get the advisor up to speed. A strong-minded executive may presume that no advisor knows as much as he does.

An effective professional advisor can, however, add immeasurably to the business success. Some of the most savvy, successful executives assert that they cannot afford to do business if they do not have the right professional advisor.

Not hiring a professional advisor can be a mistake.

69 No Consultants Allowed

Some executives and some companies refuse to work with consultants.

There may be many reasons executives and companies refuse to work with consultants: bad prior experience, disinclination to spend resources, fear of change, etc. Just as sometimes there may not be a good fit between a person and an organization, so, too, sometimes there may not be a good fit between a consultant and an organization. Merely because one person has not worked effectively in a particular organization, does that mean you would reject consideration of another person, who might work effectively in that organization? To reject consultants without objectively considering the contributions that consultants can make reflects similar thinking, and can deny you access to some of the extraordinarily positive things that consultants can add to organizations.

Rejecting consultants out of hand can be a mistake.

70 Retaining the Wrong Professional Advisor

From time to time companies and senior executives inevitably are involved in circumstances that are not familiar to them. In those circumstances, it is a good idea to retain a professional advisor. But it can be disastrous if the wrong advisor is retained.

Often the decision about the advisor who is retained is much more controlling in determining the outcome that is achieved than are the merits of the strategy pursued, the potential of the new business opportunity, what diligence is employed, or how much resources are expended. If you retain the wrong advisor, you may end up with an unfortunate outcome.

Retaining the wrong advisor is a mistake.

71 Retaining an Inexperienced Agent

With the growing complexity of business today, an agent is often retained to represent the company in a major transaction.

In selecting an agent, companies may be challenged because the very issues on which they seek representation are the ones in which they have only limited experience or background. If the agent that the company selects is similarly inexperienced, then the company will not have gained access to the experience and knowledge that it needs. The company may find that the agent is unable to provide the perspective, experience and knowledge necessary to be and effective representative.

Retaining an inexperienced agent can be a mistake.

72 Using Untrained, Inexperienced Consultants

The objective in hiring a consultant is to gain access to specialized expertise, training and experience.

When you select a consultant to assist with a complex project, you want to confirm that the consultant is thoroughly trained in all that is necessary to do that project and also has substantial real time experience in actually doing what you want. The consultant lacking in training and experience increases the risk of disappointment.

Relying upon a consultant lacking in the requisite training and experience can be a mistake.

73 Relying on the Generic Consultant

Sometimes a generic consultant—bringing a fresh perspective and no preconceived notions to the problem—is the best solution. But not always.

One appeal of generic consultants is that they often are less expensive than the highly specialized expert. But the generic consultant, lacking in-depth knowledge of the particular situation, may prove to be a much more expensive solution than the knowledgeable, experienced, specialist consultant. You may end up paying a lot for the generic consultant's learning curve. And if the generic consultant does not master the lessons well, you may pay much more in the long term than if you hired the specialist at the beginning.

Relying on the generic consultant can be a mistake.

74 Gurus at Cross Purposes

Some companies are intrigued by the idea of retaining and working with many management gurus.

The objective of working with management gurus is that their ideas will be transferred to the company in positive ways, so that the company and its people will benefit and perform better than they might, had they not been exposed to the gurus and the gurus' ideas. But too many gurus can be worse than no gurus, as their ideas may be in conflict. Ideas that may be appealing when viewed independently can be confusing when viewed interdependently. Companies can encounter the difficulty of feeding the people too many guru ideas and thereby causing intellectual indigestion.

Too many guru ideas can be a mistake.

75 Ignoring Advantages of University Contact

Some companies are so anchored in the "real world" that they ignore the advantages of university contact.

While much that occurs in the university may be perceived as peripheral and unrelated to business, university contact can provide some definite advantages. One advantage is an inside track to hiring students. Another advantage is access to faculty for training programs. Or, faculty might make a company problem the subject of a special student project, enabling the company to get access to low cost "consulting in training" project work. University contact can facilitate tracking major trends and developments, especially in the technology realm. University contact can be a source of product development and technological innovation.

Ignoring the advantages of university contact can be a mistake.

76 Thinking you Need to Own the Factory

Many companies think that if they sell products, they need to own the factory.

The old style model of business presumed that companies that made products owned the factories in which the products were made. The thinking was that since the company was all about the product it was crucial to concentrate management talent on making the product, and the best way to do that was to own the factory. Indeed, some of the great manufacturing companies, such as automobile manufacturers, evolved out of innovative ways of making things—most especially Henry Ford's pioneering assembly line. Today, however, many alternative approaches to making things can be employed. More and more, many companies that sell products don't own the plants in which the products are made. Instead, they outsource manufacturing.

Thinking that the only way a product company can make its products is to own the factory in which the products are made, can be a mistake.

77 Decentralizing a Function That Logically Can Be Centralized

Activities that have common components and attributes may be more cost-effectively performed and coordinated in a centralized way.

If activities are coordinated and centralized, it is possible to apply systems to achieve economies that would be unachievable were the activities uncoordinated. Systems and coordination can reduce costs and improve service. Improved service can lead to more repeat business and more referrals. Systems and coordination can grow revenues and profits.

Failing to centralize a function that can thereby achieve superior service and lower cost can be a mistake.

FINANCE AND ACCOUNTING

78 Success Needs Sufficient Capital Resources

To succeed in business, you need sufficient capital resources. In fact, it is said that the number one source of failure for small business is running out of money.

If you do not have a realistic assessment of the money that is needed to implement your business plan, you run the risk of running out of money. If you run out of money, your business may likely fail. Failure to have a realistic understanding of the amount of money that is required for the business overall and to implement certain new ventures, particularly, can lead to ruin.

Failing to have adequate money for the business can be a mistake.

79 Lacking a Financial Plan

Every business must have a financial plan.

While creative approaches can be employed to address shortfalls in many critical resources, the one resource no company can do without is money. If you do not plan your financial needs, you may find that the demands for money exceed the available supply. If you run short of money, you may not only lose opportunities, but also lose the business.

Failing to have a financial plan can be a mistake.

80 Failing to Create a Banking Relationship in Advance

Relationships take time to develop—and a banking relationship is no exception.

Astute executives recognize that creating banking relationships can take time. Consequently, they invest the necessary time to create the relationship. By having spent the time to create the relationship in advance, when they have banking needs the bank is more likely to respond positively, than had the initial investment to create the relationship not been made.

Failing to invest necessary time to create the banking relationship can be a mistake.

81 Relying on a Single Financing Source

Many banks insist on being a company's sole banker.

Although there are many reasons why the banker may want to be your sole banker, it is very risky for a company to bank with only one bank. If you rely upon only one bank, you may find that you are exposed to significant, unanticipated risk. What if the bank decides to stop doing business with your type of customer? What if the bank decides to change its policies or lending criteria? What if there's a change in personnel and your previous good relationship is replaced by someone who is less than sympathetic to your company and its financing needs? If you rely exclusively on one financing source, you may find yourself in trouble at the very time you need financial help.

To rely on one financing source is a mistake.

82 Asking for Money at the Wrong Time

The timing of when you ask for money can be the crucial consideration on whether or not you get the money you want.

If you ask for money when you really need it, you are less likely to have your request granted than if you ask for money when you don't need it. There's a saying that a banker is quite willing to lend you an umbrella on a sunny day but not on a rainy day. To get access to the money you need, you should ask for it when you do not need it. Then, when you need it, it will be available.

Asking for money at the wrong time can be a mistake.

83 Confusing Accounting Profit and Cash Flow

Accounting profit and cash flow are not the same thing.

Cash flow is the difference between the cash you collect and the cash you pay out. Accounting profit includes cash, but with many adjustments for non-cash items, revenues that are expected to be paid in cash at a future time but have yet to be collected, plus expenses that relate to expenditures that apply to multiple time periods and need to be assigned to the appropriate periods. Ultimately, value is created by cash flow—not accounting profits. The recent corporate financial reporting scandals and the Internet technology bubble are eloquent testimony that cash flow is what counts—not accounting profit, which is amenable to manipulation.

Thinking accounting profit and cash flow are the same thing is a mistake.

84 Playing to Wall Street

Many CEOs place a great deal of emphasis on understanding and then delivering what Wall Street wants.

The emphasis on meeting Wall Street's desires is understandable. After all, if Wall Street is dissatisfied with a company's performance, and with its CEO in particular, this dissatisfaction can result in investors selling the company's stock. If more people want to sell a stock than buy it, the price inevitably will decline. If the stock declines too much, the board will put pressure upon the CEO to deliver a higher stock price. If the CEO does not deliver the higher stock price, the CEO will be out of a job.

But emphasizing what Wall Street wants is a precarious, even dangerous way to go. It is better to emphasize a sound business strategy. Emphasizing what Wall Street wants is analogous to concentrating on the result only and ignoring how to get the result.

It can be a mistake to put too much emphasis on what Wall Street wants.

85 Too Much Concentration on the Stock Price

Some companies, especially those with stock prices the market has bid up to high levels, seem to be overly involved with the stock price.

If a company pays too much attention to the stock price, the company may lose focus on what its business is all about. The company may forget how important it is to serve its customers. The company may forget that its stock price is a function of its profitability, future prospects, and the overall soundness of its business. If the company concentrates too much on the stock price, which is a behavioral-influenced assessment of its basic performance, rather than on the factors that lead to good business outcomes, the company may find that its basic business—and subsequently its stock price—suffers.

Concentrating too much on the stock price is a mistake.

86 Excess Attention to EPS

Some managers and investors put way too much emphasis on EPS, the acronym for *earnings per share.*

A handy device for valuing companies in the stock market is the price-earnings multiple, the relationship between the company's share price and its earnings per share. The stock price would go up as a result of higher earnings and the willingness of the investment community to pay a higher multiple of those earnings. Not surprisingly, many companies seek to maximize reported EPS, and all too many investment analysts concentrate their attention on EPS. What really matters is cash flow. You look need no further than Warren Buffett, the world's second wealthiest individual and most successful investor, to find a proponent of emphasizing cash flow over EPS.

To think that EPS is more important that cash flow is a mistake.

87 Playing Earnings Expectations Game

As a company's stock price is influenced by both its reported and expected earnings, investment analysts understandably go to great lengths to discern what earnings a company is likely to report.

A primary way investment analysts discern a company's probable future earnings is to ask the chief executive officer what he or she expects their company's earnings are likely to be for the next quarter and the next year. Once the CEO answers the question about expected earnings, then that expectation becomes controlling, for there is extraordinary pressure on companies to perform at levels equal to expectations. Some companies will go to great lengths in efforts to meet analysts' earnings expectations, , even compromising primary business strategies and favoring the short-term at the expense of the long-term. Companies may cut out advertising, research and training—or even lay off needed personnel. But ultimately, the consequences of misplaced earnings priorities result in damage to the company.

To set earning targets that then cause the company to compromise its business strategy can be a mistake.

88 Ignoring the Stock Price

Companies that ignore their stock price do so at their peril.

While it is crucially important to concentrate on the basic business of the company, if a company is not mindful of what happens to its stock price, it may find it is in for a rude shock. If the stock price falls too low, investors may lose confidence in management, and critical investors may sell out. If the stock price falls too low, a takeover may happen. A company needs to pay attention both to its basic business and it its stock price.

Ignoring the company's stock price is a mistake.

89 Lacking Financial Return Targets

When a company commits capital to a new venture, it is important to have a goal for the return on investment of the capital from that venture.

It can be dangerous to proceed to commit capital, if you have no idea what return you want on that capital. Capital, after all, has a cost. Those who provide the capital expect to get a return on that capital, or, at the very least, will charge you interest for that capital. If you are not clear about what return you wish to make on the capital you invest in the new venture—which objective needs to be informed by the expectations of those who provide you the capital—then you have no way of knowing whether the venture will be successful or not.

Embarking on a new venture without a clear idea of the return on the investment objective can be a mistake.

90 Failing to Calculate Return on Investment

Sometimes, in the excitement of the promised benefits from a new investment, the actual calculation of the return that is expected from that investment is disregarded.

If the calculation of the return on investment is not made, evaluating that investment—on a stand-alone basis, in comparison to other investment opportunities, and in terms of the company's cost of capital—is not possible. Any capital commitment should be made on the basis of a careful calculation of the return on investment (ROI) expected from that capital commitment. The ROI calculation is fundamental to strategy.

Making a capital commitment without calculating the return on investment can be a mistake.

91 Investing in Projects Unrelated to Business Goals

Too often, companies make investments that are interesting in the abstract, but which have no ultimate relationship to the business's permanent goals.

Capital expenditures should have a direct linkage and relationship to business goals. Unless it is possible to demonstrate clearly, specifically, and emphatically how that investment will improve the company's performance in those areas that are the company's priorities, the company should not go ahead. Making investments unrelated to business goals means that the company is committing resources in ways that are unrelated to its desired outcomes.

To make a capital investment unrelated to business goals can be a mistake.

92 Pricing and Cost Mismatch

Some companies are confused about the imperative of matching price and cost.

If a company aspires to be the low-price seller, then it must have a cost structure to match its pricing priorities. Correspondingly, a company that offers high-priced products must incur the costs that are involved in creating quality that the high price promises.

Failing to connect price and cost and quality is a mistake.

93 Confusing Pricing Markups with Pricing Discounts

Some pricing approaches can confuse discount and markup—much to the detriment of one side of the transaction.

Consider the confusion that can ensue depending upon interpretation of how to apply a markup for retail value above costs. Considering a 30% markup and $13 million of inventory cost, one approach might be to suggest that the relevant cost figure would be $9.1 million, which is 70% of $13 million. But an alternative calculation would say that the relevant figure is $10 million, for 130% of that number is $13 million. The $10 million figure is about 77% of 13 million. The difference is whether pricing is approached from the perspective of a 30% markup or a 30% discount.

Confusion concerning pricing markups and pricing discounts can result in an expensive mistake.

94 First Spending the Money then Figuring Out How To Pay for It

When embarking upon a new venture, the temptation is strong to address all that you want to do and should do.

What you want to do and should do costs money. No small number of companies rush out and spend money on what they want to do and should do, and only later stop to figure out how they might get the money to pay for it. Unless the source of money is confirmed to be available, you may never get to do all that you want to do and should do, because you ran out of money. This, in sum, is the story of how many new economy dot.com companies became dot.bomb companies.

It is a mistake to rush out to spend money before you figure out how you will pay for it.

95 Misperceived Role of Risk in Assessing Financial Commitments

Companies engaged in negotiations of major decisions understandably place particular emphasis on the magnitude of the financial commitments. The risk context of significant decisions should be carefully considered.

A substantial decision involving a significant financial commitment made absent consideration of the context of risk is susceptible to miscalculation. A payment that is dependent upon an outcome being achieved has a very different value than a payment that is guaranteed. A level of compensation that may be very appropriate for a certain level of business performance being delivered could be highly inappropriate if that payment is guaranteed independent of business performance. What may be fully appropriate in a high-risk environment may be entirely inappropriate in a low-risk environment.

A substantial commitment made without sufficient consideration of the risk context of that decision may result in a mistake.

96 Using Profit for ROI Calculations

The calculation of ROI—acronym for *return on investment*—can be a perilous undertaking.

The purpose of the ROI calculation is to measure what return is really received. Profit can be ephemeral—it may be received or it may not. Profit cannot be spent, cannot be used to make another reinvestment, and cannot be put in the bank. Cash can be spent, invested and deposited in the bank. If you want to do an accurate ROI analysis, you use cash flows, not profit.

Thinking profit is what you should use in calculating ROI is a mistake.

97 Misapplication of Economic Value Added Concept

Many companies have embraced the notion that the economic-value-added concept is superior to the traditional performance assessment measures based on traditional accounting.

Economic value added, known by the acronym EVA, is a financial measurement metric that considers the relationship between the enterprise's profitability and the cost of the capital employed to achieve that profitability. The idea behind EVA is that managers should be evaluated in terms of how effectively, productively and profitably they employ capital in the business. To evaluate profit alone without considering the cost of the capital employed to achieve that profit can be very misleading. But if the relevant content and timing factors are not appropriately considered, EVA calculations can be as distorting and misleading as traditional profitability measures.

In one instance, a comparison of an EVA calculation of a real estate development venture to an EVA calculation of a consumer finance activity was severely flawed because the differing contexts and time horizons of the two businesses were not sufficiently considered in the EVA analyses.

Relying on a misapplication of EVA performance assessment can be a mistake.

98 Confusing Volume with Profit

Many companies have the attitude that if they achieve enough volume, profits will take care of themselves.

At the end of the day profit is the primary financial metric of concern to a business. If your business is fixated on what will maximize profit, you have a far better prospect of achieving your desired profit objectives than if your business if fixated upon volume. Although a larger volume business will generate more profits than a smaller business with the same profit margin, if you do not confirm that the business is profitable, volume alone will not get you there.

Emphasizing volume rather than profits can be a mistake.

99 Disregarding Importance of Economic Environment

A company's ability to be successful is very much a function of the economic environment in which it operates.

If a company is operating in a very difficult, challenging economic environment its chances of achieving outstanding business performance are fundamentally constrained by the condition of the economy. As long as the economy is difficult, the company's chances of achieving outstanding results, from a business as usual approach, are going to be limited. In certain circumstances, the company may want to consider redirecting its business to those products or service offers that may be more positively received in that economy, allocating resources to markets in other economies that are not constrained by the difficult home economy, and/or advocating public policies to improve the economy.

To consider business as usual, irrespective of the condition of the economy, is a mistake.

100 Refusing to Spend Money to Make Money

Some companies, when faced with financial pressures, cut spending.

The thinking behind cutting spending, when faced with financial pressures, is the imperative to reduce out-going expenses and husband financial reserves. As important as cost containment can be, there is a maxim in business that you have to spend money to make money. Indeed, a major motivation for company spending is to invest in tools of production to reduce costs of production rather than to expand output. Companies unwilling to make such expenditures may be unable to reduce costs.

To decline to spend money to make money can be a mistake.

101 Forgetting to Confirm That You Are Actually Using All That You Are Paying For

In business it can be all too easy for there to be a disconnect between what is paid for and what is actually used.

Just because a business pays for something doesn't mean that it is actually used. It can be all too easy for a payment arrangement to become institutionalized, to become part of ongoing regular procedures, and a standard feature of the budget. But it may be that what is being paid for is no longer utilized. Maybe what is being paid for served the needs of an activity or division or individual that is no longer involved in the company. Just because you are paying for something does not necessarily mean you are using it.

Paying for something that you don't actually use is a mistake.

102 Too Much Legacy Expense

Legacy expenses are those expenses that derive from prior activities and prior investments, rather than present business and investments for the future.

Legacy expenses reflect decisions made in the past and obligations undertaken in the past. Companies that have disproportionate legacy expenses, relative to the present and future, are at a significant competitive disadvantage to those that are not similarly burdened. If disproportionate resources are spent paying for the past, relative to the present and the future, the capability of the company to be effective is compromised.

Too much legacy expense is a mistake.

103 Expending too Many Resources on Problems

It has been said that business is all about solving problems.

Superior executives are superior because of their ability to solve problems. But problem-solving is not the only thing that business is about. Business also involves identifying and exploiting opportunities. Peter Drucker once observed that companies should survive problems and concentrate on opportunities. If you spend too many resources on problems, you may not have sufficient resources remaining to pursue opportunities.

Spending too many resources on problems can be a mistake.

104 Miscomprehending Direct Costs

Many in business miscomprehend the difference between direct costs and full costs.

Direct costs are the incremental costs involved in delivering a product or delivering a service. Direct costs are the costs involved in adding additional units of production or service delivery, as contrasted to full cost, which includes not only the incremental direct costs, but also other costs including investment return, overhead expenses not directly related to that transaction, and the capital invested in that particular venture. In some instances, full costs are much higher than direct costs, sometimes many multiples higher. Decisions made without comprehension of full costs can lead to bad decisions.

If you do not understand the difference between direct costs and full costs, you may be making a mistake.

105 Decision Based on Weak Cost Information

Many companies operate with weak cost information.

If your cost information is weak, your decisions may be weak. If you do not know what your costs are for different volumes of business, different product lines, different times of the year, and different circumstances and conditions, you may make decisions that are very different than the decisions you would make, if you had that knowledge. Strong cost information is crucial to effective business decisions.

Making decisions on the basis of weak cost information is a mistake.

106 Confused by Sunk Costs

Economic theory holds that sunk costs can be irrelevant to decision making.

Sunk costs are those costs that are already spent and therefore cannot be recovered. The idea behind the irrelevancy of sunk costs for decision making is that one should consider only incremental costs and benefits from this point forward. Decision making should be based on a forward-looking rather than backward-looking perspective.

To concentrate on that which has already been spent and cannot be recovered, is a mistake.

PURCHASING AND SUPPLY CHAIN

107 Too Much Emphasis on Low Price

Many factors are important in purchasing—not just price.

Everyone wants to get the best deal possible. No surprises here. But sometimes searching for the best deal possible can be a mistake, if it leads to spending excessive time searching for that best deal. Though low price is appealing on the surface, because everyone would rather pay less for something, if a company does not bother to consider why the price is so low, the company may find it is for a surprise. Generally speaking, you get what you pay for. If the company does not investigate what additional costs or risks it may be incurring with the low price, it may find it is in for a very expensive surprise—and may have to spend more money in the end to replace faulty or not-up-to-par purchases.

Emphasizing price at the expense of overall functionality and quality can be a mistake.

108 Too Much Emphasis on Purchase Price and Not on Terms

A purchase involves consideration of not only the purchase price but the terms associated with the purchase price.

If you are buying something, a higher price with advantageous terms may be a better deal than a low price. Depending upon the terms, the timing of payment may make the effective price much lower than the nominal price, especially if you're able to enjoy the time value of money benefit of deferring when you have to pay for what you buy. Further, if significant service and additional benefits are bundled with the transaction—which if sold unbundled would cost substantially more—it may be worthwhile to pay a higher price and get more, than to pay a lower price and get less.

Putting too much emphasis on purchase price without considering the importance of terms is a mistake.

109 Buying at Less Than Cost

Some companies have the idea that if you can buy something at less than cost, that is a great deal.

Sometimes, buying at less than cost is an excellent way to go. But what if what you pay, even if it is less than cost, is still above the value of what you are acquiring? While "cost" is the sum of the expenditures the producer or purchaser incurred, it does not reflect market value, which is what someone else would actually pay. Just because you can buy something for less than cost does not necessarily mean it's a good deal. Smart managers know that more discrimination is needed, beyond the standard of just buying at less than cost.

Buying at less than cost can be a mistake.

110 Relying on Low-Cost Service Contract

Selecting a low-cost service arrangement can be a tempting way to economize.

Consider the retailer that bought an expensive, complex system. Once the system was up and working, the store chose to rely upon an independent service arrangement. However, when the sole proprietor of that service enterprise became sick and unable to work, at the very time the State mandated a one-week sales tax moratorium on certain products—requiring all retailers to adjust how they accounted for and charged sales tax—the retailer was thrown into a crisis, whose solution proved to be very expensive.

Sometimes the low-cost service provider can be a short-term false economy—long-term expensive mistake.

111 Sacrificing for Low Cost

The primary consideration driving many business decisions is cost.

What all too many executives do not appreciate is that the quest for lowest cost can in fact involve significant cost. How so? To achieve lowest cost, a company may move manufacturing far from the point of sale. Then, getting the products from where they are made to where they are sold may involve greater costs than if sales and production were located nearby. Furthermore, by emphasizing cost, the company may be forced to compromise other important customer priorities.

To fail to appreciate the consequences of all of the costs involved in low-cost business decisions can be a mistake.

112 Believing the Quoted Price Is the Price You Should Pay

Many people have the idea that the price that is quoted is the price they should pay.

The price that is quoted is nothing more than the price that the merchant would like to receive. It may be that it is a fair price, but perhaps the price that is quoted is not the price you should pay. Every price is susceptible to negotiation. Certainly, the tendency is to accept the asking price without question. But many sellers will, if asked, negotiate a better deal than the asking price. If you don't ask, you will never discover what price you might have gotten.

To think that the price that is asked is the price you should pay is a mistake.

113 Not Distinguishing between Easy-to-Buy and Easy-to-Use

In business, you need to not only buy things, but you have to use them.

Merely because something may be easier to buy—because of advantageous pricing, flexible terms, or accommodating customer service—does not necessarily mean it is easy to use. Sometimes, the products or services that are harder to buy but easier to use are the better alternative.

Easy-to-buy products and services do not usually take into account the customer's need to carefully assess their current requirements, anticipate future requirements, or consider alternatives. A vendor who insists on the customer spending more time assessing explicit present needs, future requirements, and different alternatives imposes more cost and effort—but often more up-front effort results in a much better outcome.

Easy-to-buy can be a mistake.

114 Relying on Crony Capitalism Rather Than Market Reality

In some cultures crony capitalism—doing business deals with your cronies on a "you scratch my back, I'll scratch your back" basis—is the essence of the economy.

Although crony capitalism can be appealing at one level, ultimately crony capitalism is self-dealing in a closed system. Crony capitalism can be disconnected from market reality, as transactions are justified on the basis of personal relationships rather than dollars and cents. Companies that rely primarily upon crony capitalism are quite susceptible to encountering disappointments.

To rely on crony capitalism rather than market reality can be a mistake.

115 Ignoring Supply Chain Interdependencies

The supply chain is a basic model for thinking about what is involved in getting goods and services to your customers.

The supply chain concept considers the different players and contributors that collectively make up the steps in producing and delivering products and services to customers. The supply chain starts with the raw materials, then leads to the different companies that process those raw materials, then to the company that processes, packages, and prepares the final product and service for the customer. Companies that excel generally do so because they have outstanding supply chain management, either by happenstance or, more often, by conscious attention. Companies that have problems often have problems somewhere along the supply chain. If you want to excel in business, you need to excel in supply chain management.

To fail to pay sufficient attention to supply chain issues can be a mistake.

116 Selecting a Supply Chain Model That Results in Limited Restocking Capabilities in a Rapidly Shifting Market

The supply chain model that a company selects inevitably determines its capabilities to respond to shifting customer preferences and desires.

If a company operates in a business in which preferences and desires change rapidly—such as women's fashion—the supply chain model determines how quickly the company can respond to shifting patterns. When manufacturing is outsourced, the capability respond quickly to shifting patterns is limited. With outsourced manufacturing, most fashion retailers bring in new merchandise once or perhaps twice in a season. This rigid supply chain model inherently limits the capability of a store to respond to style shifts. But if manufacturing and design are internally integrated and controlled, many restocking cycles within a season are possible. A store that can restock multiple times within the season has a competitive advantage over those stores that cannot.

To rely on a rigid supply chain model that limits the capabilities to respond to market shifts can be a mistake.

117 Too Little Concern with Logistics

Ultimately, every strategy idea needs to be implemented. Implementation inevitably involves logistics.

Logistics is all about the many tasks and considerations involved in moving products and goods between buyer and seller, supplier and processor, producer and user. Logistics considerations include physical movement of goods from place to place and all of the related communications, information, organizational and regulatory issues associated with such movement. To excel in business, you need to pay attention to logistics. If you do not pay attention to logistics, your prospects of excelling in business may be jeopardized.

To fail to pay appropriate attention to logistics can be a mistake.

118 Building up Too Much Inventory in Anticipation of Sales That Never Occur

In many businesses, the goods are made by the manufacturer and bought by the merchant before the customer actually buys them.

If you miscalculate in forecasting what manufacturing activity is needed to meet customers' orders, you may build up excess inventory. If the company believes that every order is a likely sale, production, which necessarily starts with a long lead time, may result in excess, unneeded, and very expensive inventory. In fact, this is what happened to SYSCO in 2001, when its much heralded instantaneous financial reporting system proved unreliable, causing the company to take an unprecedented two-billion-dollar-plus inventory write-off.

Building up too much inventory in anticipation of sales that never occur can be a mistake.

119 There's One Best Brand

Many companies promote the idea that there is one best brand.

Although in some market segments one single brand may emerge to be the dominant, acknowledged, and accepted "best brand," in many markets multiple brands compete for customers' patronage. One brand may appeal to a particular set of customer needs while a different brand may appeal to a different set of customer needs. To think that there is one best brand, superior to every other brand, flies in the face of customer experiences and market realities.

To embrace the idea that there is one best brand may be a mistake.

120 Excessive Reliance on One-stop Shopping

In today's fast-paced, overly complicated world, the appeal of one-stop shopping is great: rather than having to go to many different shops to get what you need, you can go to one shop and get it all.

In many instances, one-stop shopping is an excellent solution. But not in every instance. Sometimes the product that is available from the one shop where you can purchase other things is nowhere nearly as useful, valuable, or appropriate as the product that could be available if you went to a specialty shop. As a case in point, the range of choices and quality of options in a top-end bicycle shop—in terms of frames, components, wheels, clothing, and equipment, plus knowledgeable and capable customer service—is vastly superior to what is available at a general sporting goods store.

Putting too much reliance on one-stop shopping can be a mistake.

121 Excessive Reliance on One Supplier

If a company depends exclusively upon a single supplier, that company is at risk if anything happens to that supplier.

What if a supplier goes out of business? What if the supplier's quality and service decline precipitously, compromising the company's ability to meet its own expectations and commitments to its customers? What if the supplier decides to redirect its business, jettisoning customers that no longer serve its priorities? If it turns out that your company is one of the customers left behind, then how will your company cope?

To put exclusive reliance upon a single supplier is a mistake.

122 Dealing with Dealers Who Don't Know the Vendor's Products

While a dealer can be an invaluable ally, sometimes the dealer doesn't really know enough.

Consider the problem of a retailer who bought its computer from one vendor, then bought its software from a dealer who turned out to know very little about how the software worked. When the system didn't work, no one had an overall, integrated viewpoint on how to solve the problem.

To deal with a dealer who doesn't know the vendor's products can be a mistake.

STYLES AND PRIORITIES

123 No Checks and Balances

The concept of checks and balances—one part of an organization checking and balancing another part—is central to managerial practice.

Checks and balances are effectively applied in both the public and private sectors. In the United States the three branches of government—executive, legislative and judicial—act to check and balance each other, so that no one of the three exerts too much influence and dominance. The same approach applies in business. If you lack a checks and balances system, you may discover that one part of the organization is exerting disproportionate influence, to the disadvantage of the corporation's ultimate performance and well being.

If you fail to employ appropriate checks and balances in your management systems and practices, you may be making a mistake.

124 Inappropriate Integration of Decision Authority

Companies whose decision making authority is inappropriately integrated are often inviting a disaster to happen.

Separation of power is fundamental to good governance—both in the public realm and in private enterprise. Just as the United States Constitution provides for three branches of government, so too should private corporations provide three branches of authority for decisions involving commitments of the enterprise's resources. Good corporate governance involves separating the people and business units that are involved in (1) creating a new business idea, venture, service or product, or investment opportunity; (2) evaluating the merits of the commitment; and (3) approving the commitment of the enterprise's resources. When the three functions of initiating, evaluating and approving are combined and integrated into a single business unit, the quality of the decisions may suffer. Many corporate scandals—such as those at Enron, Tyco and WorldCom—resulted from a lack of separation of initiating, evaluating and approving.

To combine initiating, evaluating and approving a commitment of corporate resources in a single individual business unit is a mistake.

125 Too Far Removed from the Field

Modern organizations utilize multiple levels of management to oversee, coordinate and integrate specialized functions within the company and far-flung production and customer operations.

If the ultimate decision-makers are too far removed from the customers and the people in the field who actually do the work, the company's decisions may be made by people who have minimal, if any, first-hand knowledge of customers' concerns and operational realities. If decision-makers are too far removed from the field, their decisions may be characterized by insensitivity, misinformation and a lack of appreciation for nuance, timing, and competitive conditions.

To have important decisions made by those who are too far removed from the field can be a mistake.

126 Paying Too Little Attention to Process

As important as outcomes are, if the means by which the outcome is achieved are not sufficiently considered, the consequences can be severe.

One benefit of emphasizing process is the resulting replicable approach to doing a particular task. Understanding how an outcome was achieved results in the capacity to replicate that outcome. If result alone is emphasized, then the ability to accomplish that result in the future may be limited to non-existent.

A major downside of paying too little attention to process is that people may resort to any means to accomplish a desired outcome. If the process is not given enough attention, so that the outcome is achieved by unreliable or even nefarious means, the consequences may be severely negative.

Paying too little attention to process is a mistake.

127 Emphasizing Assessment of Process Performance Over Process Appropriateness

In evaluating a business activity, a critical question is the appropriateness of a process, rather than how well the process itself is performed.

All too often there can be a tendency to emphasize the performance of a particular process. Although process performance is important, it is subordinate to process appropriateness. If the right process is not being performed, how well it is being performed is of much less importance.

To emphasize process performance at the expense of process appropriateness is a mistake.

128 Emphasizing Process Over Outcomes

In many settings, the means by which something happens is given as much attention as what actually happens.

Process is important. If a company does not have an understanding of how an outcome was achieved and the capacity to replicate that outcome, then the company's prospects are much compromised. However, emphasizing process at the expense of outcome is equally inappropriate. As important as process is, process exists to serve outcomes, not to serve itself.

To emphasize process at the expense of outcomes is a mistake.

129 Closed-Minded Thinking

In today's tumultuous business environment, executives are challenged by the bombardment of new information, ideas, threats and opportunities. Such circumstances require a sense of curiosity, an open mind, and the inclination to consider challenging ideas.

If a company is too close-minded, being so self-referential that it is unwilling and unable to consider other points of view, it will be less than effective. A company that is too close-minded will miss opportunities. Even worse, the company may ignore threats that could lead to its destruction.

Being too closed-minded is a mistake.

130 Rigidly Insisting Upon a Single Methodology

Some companies identify a decision making methodology they like and then insist that that methodology be used for every decision.

By using the right decision methodology, you increase the chances of making better decisions. As long as all of the decisions a company might face are the same decisions, then getting the right methodology and insisting on consistent application may be the best way to go. But what if the company's decisions are not all the same? What if one best decision methodology is not really the best for every decision?

Insisting upon using one decision methodology, irrespective of the decisions to be made, can be a mistake.

131 Inflexibility

While confidence in your opinions and commitment to your position can be commendable, if taken too far—to the point of inflexibility—the company may suffer.

Inflexibility means that a company is unreceptive to exploring a different way of doing things—even if that different way may be a better way. Inflexibility means that the company presumes it has a monopoly on the best approach. Others may be able to suggest an adaptation or modification of the company's approach that improves a company's position. But the company that clings to inflexibility will never know.

Inflexibility can be a mistake.

132 Discounting Role of Creativity in Business

Creativity is central to business success.

Creativity involves bringing into existence something that did not previously exist. Peter Drucker observed that the purpose of business is to *create* and maintain customers. Creativity permeates all aspects of business—creating customer relationships, creating products, creating solutions to customer problems. Creativity can improve product offers, solve problems and delight customers. Certainly creativity is an essential core competence of entrepreneurs. Arguably, creativity is a critical success factor for business survival. A company that does not encourage creativity does so at its peril.

Discounting the importance of creativity is a mistake.

133 Disproportionate Emphasis on Creativity

Since many business strategists have identified innovation as *the* crucial business success ingredient in the twenty-first century, many executives believe that they must place primary emphasis on creativity.

As important as creativity is, too much creativity may be as bad as—or even worse than—no creativity. Setting aside the personal enjoyment that can come from the experience and expression of creativity, creating something anew may be much more expensive and much less effective than buying or adapting what has already been created. As a case in point, adapting a proven headline and advertising campaign to your particular circumstances and purposes may be a much more cost-effective and financially rewarding approach than creating something from scratch. A new advertising campaign and headline may involve significantly greater costs than adapting what has already been proven to work successfully—and you also do not know whether the new campaign will be successful.

While creativity is important, disproportionate emphasis on creativity may be a mistake.

134 Too Little *Gravitas*

In a business environment in which reliability and trust are increasingly important, *gravitas* more and more is a prerequisite.

Although some companies may talk about having high standards and emphasize the importance of competence, you would not know it to observe the type of people they pick for certain important positions. If *gravitas*, high seriousness, is important to the business model—but somehow the company does not seem to manifest *gravitas* in how it actually goes about doing what it does—the disconnect between the projected image and reality may be painfully evident. Without sufficient *gravitas*, the company may not do that well.

Lacking needed *gravitas* can be a mistake.

135 Playing Not to Lose Rather Than Playing to Win

Some companies employ an overly defensive style of decision making.

The defensive style of decision making emphasizes not making mistakes: playing not to lose rather than playing to win. But in a competitive endeavor, you must play offense as well as defense. In a soccer game, if all you do is concentrate on being sure the other side never scores a goal, while you do not make much effort to score goals on your own, the best you can hope for is a tie. As important as defense is, you must also play offense.

Playing defense exclusively is a mistake.

136 Rules Dominate Relationship

Businesses often have to choose whether to prioritize rules or the relationship.

Rules are established to achieve consistency and uniformity in decisions. Without rules, decisions might be made on an ad hoc basis, in ways that serve neither the business nor its customers. But if rules get in the way of a customer relationship, the company needs to decide whether its rules or its customer relationships are more important. How this matter is decided can determine how successful the company might be. Companies that steadfastly stick to rules are destined for mediocrity or worse.

Prioritizing rules over relationships is a mistake.

137 Not Offending People

Some companies are insistent that they not do anything that would be offensive to anyone.

Certainly, it is preferred not to engage in inappropriate, overtly offensive behavior. But if you were to identify every thing you might do that could possibly be offensive to someone, it could be a pretty long list. And some of the items on that list might be excellent strategic initiatives, which could have a very positive impact upon your business. But if you are more concerned with not offending someone than with having a positive impact on your business, you may choose to sacrifice the positive business outcome.

To choose not to offend someone over a positive impact on your business can be a mistake.

138 Refusal To Negotiate

Some companies take the attitude that they will not negotiate.

Refusal to negotiate is, in fact, a negotiating tactic. The company that refuses to negotiate is saying that it will not consider the other side's needs or circumstances. Refusing to negotiate could preclude the opportunity to consider what might possibly be a more creative approach that may benefit everyone, including the other side, at no cost to the company, or even an alternative that might enhance the company's position. If a company refuses to negotiate, it may lose out on the chance for a much-improved set of circumstances.

Refusal to negotiate can be a mistake.

139 Everything Is Negotiable

Some companies adopt the attitude that everything is negotiable.

The *everything is negotiable* attitude can be problematic, if there is no foundation, no unmoving point of reference, or no anchor to the company's position. If everything is always a moving target, if the company is always willing to negotiate, if the company never takes a stand and sticks to it, then people with whom the company interacts have no reason not to continue to ask to negotiate. Negotiations go on and on, virtually without end. A company can spend so much time negotiating that it doesn't get much done. And, by being so open to negotiation, the company does not get nearly as good of a deal on important issues, as if it were to take a stand.

Adopting an attitude that *everything is negotiable* can be a mistake.

140 Big Hat, No Cattle

In Texas, if you emphasize form over substance, if you suggest that you have more capability and resources than you really possess, your behavior may be labeled *big hat, no cattle.*

Big hat, no cattle approaches can cause companies to emphasize appearance over reality. But while appearances do count, if there is no substance behind the appearance—if there are not enough cattle to go along with the big hat—the likelihood of eventually getting enough cattle in the herd is not very great. Had the emphasis placed on appearances been directed to the reality, eventually you could have the herd of cattle to go along with the size of the hat you want to wear.

Big hat, no cattle can be a mistake.

141 Image Ambiguity

If a company's image is characterized more by ambiguity than by clarity, then the company may not be nearly as effective as it could be.

If a company's image is ambiguous—messages and impressions that are sent to the public are confusing, contradictory and inconsistent—then people will not know what to think, what is expected of them, what they should do. Although ambiguity may be favored in some situations, when it comes to image, clarity is much preferred. Without clarity, the company lacks focus and performance inevitably suffers.

An ambiguous company image is a mistake.

142 *Not-Invented-Here* Syndrome

Some companies have such a strong self-referential orientation that they will only consider ideas and innovation that they themselves create.

The *not-invented-here* syndrome can be dangerous. *Not-invented-here* thinking encourages intellectual inbreeding, suppresses receptivity to new ideas, and constrains innovation. Companies that operate with *a not-invented-here* approach to business find, in time, that they lag competitors that have more open attitudes to new ideas.

Not-invented-here thinking can be a major mistake.

143 No Outside Input Needed

Some companies operate on the basis that they do not need to have any input from outside sources.

Companies that believe they do not need any input from outside sources operate with what could charitably be called a high degree of self-confidence—but what more accurately could be described as a resistance to new thinking. If you limit your thinking only to that which originates within the company, you necessarily limit the quality, quantity, depth, breadth, and dimensions of ideas that may be considered by your company. As a consequence, you limit innovation and thereby constrain progress.

Not to consider outside input is a mistake.

144 Failing to Test

In introducing a new sales idea—be it a product, marketing campaign, or a specific advertisement—it can pay to test.

Testing involves seeing how real people in real market conditions respond to the new idea. Testing can garner feedback concerning whether an idea works at all, how well it works, and how it compares to other ideas. Testing can allow companies to discover which approaches offer the highest returns and which approaches are uneconomic. Testing can both reduce risk and increase the bottom line.

To fail to test can be a mistake.

145 Too Much Testing

As important and valuable as testing can be, too much testing can be as bad or worse than no testing.

Some companies are so enamored of testing that they test this, test that, and test this other thing, over and over again. These companies spend so much time and money testing that they never get around to rolling out products. While they are testing, markets change, competitors gain market share, and nothing ever really gets completed.

Too much testing can be a mistake.

146 Canceling a Venture Based on One Negative Test

One of the real challenges in testing is to know when one test is enough and when one test is not enough.

Some companies may cancel a new idea based on just one test. Sometimes, one test is all it takes to glean the information that you need to make an informed decision. But in other instances, it may be appropriate to undertake multiple tests—to vary some of the critical features, communication methods and target markets. If you do more than one test, you may find that you can learn things that can enable the new idea to be wildly successful. But if you didn't do more than one test, you would never know.

To cancel a new idea after only one test is a mistake.

MANAGEMENT BEHAVIOR

147 Lack of Persistence

If lack of persistence becomes a company's cultural norm, the company may be in trouble.

Lack of persistence means that the company's business units and its people do not honor and practice persistence. If they do not achieve their objectives relatively promptly, then they lose interest and redirect their energies elsewhere. But some of the most important outcomes in business are achieved only through relentless, unwavering, undistractable persistence. If lack of persistence is a cultural norm, the company may be limiting what it could achieve.

Lack of persistence can be a mistake.

148 Absentee Management

If managers are absent from the scene of what they are responsible for managing, their effectiveness is inherently compromised

Absentee management refers to managers that are "absent"—not necessarily physically, but in terms of their involvement and caring. Managing means to be involved, to monitor, evaluate, and care. Although physical presence is usually part of managing, many managers very effectively guide organizations while physically being in other locations.

Absentee management is a mistake.

149 Lack of Follow-through

In business, if you don't follow through, you may not get the results you want.

Follow-through is critical to achieving outstanding performance. If lack of follow-through is allowed to become a cultural norm, a company's prospects of achieving its desired outcomes are compromised. If you do not have follow-through, you cannot achieve outstanding results.

Lack of follow-through can be a mistake.

150 Myopic Management

Some managers are too focused on the small details of their business to comprehend the larger picture.

Myopic management reflects a smaller, more limited view of the business and its possibilities. Harvard emeritus professor Ted Levitt, in his "Marketing Myopia" article in *Harvard Business Review*, tells of the railroad companies thinking they were in the railroad business rather than the transportation business, and thereby failing to take into account the new technology of airplanes.

Myopic management is a mistake.

151 Too Aloof

Some companies adopt a rather aloof attitude.

The aloof company is distant, inaccessible, and basically unwelcoming to others. If you are not part of the inside circle, then it is hard to even get the time of day from such companies. If the company is too aloof, it is essentially telling the market that it does not need new customers and new relationships. The company is telling the market that it is very comfortable with the status quo. If preserving the status quo and not attracting new customers is what the company wishes to do, then an aloof approach may be appropriate. But if the company is too aloof, it may not be able to achieve what it aspires to achieve.

Being too aloof is a mistake.

152 Too Familiar

Some companies have a very familiar, approachable, accessible style.

A familiar approach and accessible style may be quite appropriate in certain circumstances. But in other circumstances, a too familiar style may be highly inappropriate and may be off-putting to both existing and prospective customers. The company that is too familiar may find that rather than attracting customers, excessive familiarity causes it to lose customers.

Being too familiar can be a mistake.

153 Disconnect between Avowed Beliefs and Action

Companies that profess to believe something but then act in ways contrary to their professed beliefs send mixed messages to the marketplace.

If there is a disconnect between belief and action, customers, employees, suppliers, shareholders and the community may become skeptical, even confused. Because actions speak so much louder than words, people make judgements based on actions. No matter how much the company professes that it really believes something different than what people's judgements may be, the words will all be to no avail.

A disconnect between beliefs and actions is a mistake.

154 Failing to Read the Fine Print

If you do not have a policy of carefully reading the fine print—and adhering unwaveringly to that policy—you may get in big trouble.

If you fail to read the fine print, you may find that what you thought you had agreed to is not what you agreed to at all. You may find that you took on obligations that you did not really understand. You may find that you were counting on the other side to do something that was essentially waived or eliminated in the fine print. You may find that the essence of a deal, once all of the fine print is considered, is very different than what you really thought.

Recently a company hired an online organization to create and distribute graphical e-mail content for them. Later, to their distress, they found out that the fine print allowed the online organization to "own" the mailing lists they had given them, and to use them for their own purposes. The company had to go to a great deal of effort and expense to get out of their contract with the online organization.

If you fail to read the fine print, you make a mistake.

155 Adopting Management Fads

Some companies and their leaders are entranced by management fads.

Management fads are ideas that capture the fancy of the business community at a particular point in time. In a way, management fads are the business equivalent of Andy Warhol's pronouncement that "everyone is destined to be famous for 15 minutes." Some management ideas that start out as management fads turn into lasting management wisdom—but the majority do not.

Too much attention to management fads of short-lived significance can be a mistake.

156 Moving from Management Fad to Management Fad

Some company leaders have a propensity to move their attention from one management fad to another.

Wanting to be current and up-to-date, these leaders assiduously track new management fads. As soon as a management fad is introduced and gains a following, these leaders insist that their company adopt that management fad. The people in the company are constantly bombarded with new programs, new initiatives, and new training. Some of it is interesting, perhaps even useful. On balance, however, much of it is distracting and less than useful, demanding precious resources that could otherwise be spent on the company's business.

Moving from one management fad to another is a mistake.

157 Addicted to Chaos

Many people get so involved in a frenetic, less-than balanced approach to life that chaos, rather than order, rules the day. For some, they can be so into chaos they are addicted to it.

In some settings and circumstances, for a discrete period of time, chaos can be energizing, exciting and even a source of great creativity and reward. But as a lifestyle or as a permanent way of being, chaos is ultimately negative, defeating, and limiting. If chaos becomes too much a way of life, even to the point of addiction, the ability to be effective is lessened and quality of life is negatively impacted.

Addiction to chaos is a mistake.

158 Expecting Rather Than Inspecting

Strategy is all about converting desired outcomes into results.

How do you get the outcome you desire? To begin, you need to be clear about what outcome you actually desire. Then you need to communicate that desired outcome to those, inside and outside of the organization, who can influence its realization. This communication and the attitudes and activities around this communication create the expectation of that desired outcome. But it is not enough merely to *expect* the desired outcome. Unless you follow up your expectations with specific, explicit actions—specifically, unless you *inspect,* to backup what you *expect*—you will more often than not, find that expectations are unrealized. To get what you want, you need to inspect as well expect.

To expect but not to inspect can be a mistake.

159 Failing To Monitor Work

Workers who are monitored are more productive than those who are not.

The classic Hawthorne experiments—which tested how different production techniques and management methods affected manufacturing productivity—employed time and motion studies of assembly line production processes to determine which assembly technique yielded the highest payoff. The conclusion of the Hawthorne research was that being observed or monitored was the most significant factor influencing productivity—not the particular assembly techniques that were specified. The Hawthorne effect has broad application, for any task that is monitored and observed tends to be performed at a higher level of efficiency, effectiveness and productivity.

Failing to monitor worker productivity is a mistake.

160 Excessive Focus

Business gurus assert that focus is crucial to business success.

Concentration of effort on a task can lead to a better outcome than if effort is unfocused or dissipated. If a company cannot focus its resources, it cannot be nearly as successful as if it were able to focus its resources. But too much focus can be as much or more of a problem than too little focus. If a company is so focused that it cannot see the forest for the trees, that it cannot identify new opportunities or impending threats, then the company may suffer.

Too much focus can be a mistake.

161 Too Little Focus

In times of change, people are bombarded with new ideas, new opportunities, and new ways of thinking about and doing business.

All of the change and newness of the today's times can be seductive. But as important as it is to pay attention to new developments and to reassess whether what was done in the past may be appropriate for the future, if the company is not sufficiently focused on the tasks at hand, it may suffer. Too little focus can have terrible consequences, for what needs to get done, doesn't get done.

To have too little focus can be a mistake.

162 Giving Up Too Soon

Sometimes, if results are not immediately forthcoming, there is a temptation to quit.

One of the most important attributes of successful individuals is persistence and refusing to give in—or to give up. British Prime Minister Winston Churchill said it well: "Never quit! Never quit!" In many activities, sustained, prolonged, relentless patience and persistence are required for success. In some advertising campaigns, it takes many months before results can be achieved. Selling may require five or eight or ten or even more communications before the sale can be made. If you stop too soon, you lose the payoff that can be realized from sustained, persistent effort.

To stop too soon in the face of initial disappointment can be a strategic mistake.

163 Giving up Too Late

As important as persistence is to making a success of any challenging endeavor, it is also important to know when to give up.

There are circumstances in which refusing to quit can be a mistake. Giving up too late can cause a company to throw good money after bad, to apply excessive resources to a losing cause.

It can be a mistake to give up too late.

164 Fire-Fire-Fire—Aim and Get Ready

In precision shooting the process is ready-aim-fire. Yet some businesses question whether it is important to aim at all, favoring fire-fire-fire, before getting ready and aiming.

The tension between thoughtful preparation and action is captured well in the carpenter's rule: measure twice, cut once. If you just start cutting without measuring, you will get a lot more wood cut—but will it be cut the way you want it to be cut? Will it be usable? How much will have to be discarded?

To ignore the importance of getting ready and aiming, before you fire, can be a mistake.

168 Addressing Conflicts in Context of Time-Sensitive Circumstances

A conflict addressed in circumstances where a resolution is needed by a certain deadline, or where one party perceives there is some time urgency, can result in problematic outcomes.

If you are under time pressure, you have fewer options, less flexibility and a weakened negotiating position than if time is not a problem. If a conflict must be addressed and resolved within a constrained time, the negotiating positions of the parties might be different than they would be without the time pressure, and as a consequence the overall quality of the deal or the outcome for one or more of the parties may be diminished. It is better, when possible, to address conflicts in circumstances in which time sensitivity will not be an adverse influence.

It can be a mistake to address conflict in the context of time-sensitive circumstances.

166 Doing What You Want and Ignoring the Consequences

Some companies operate with a rather imperial attitude, believing and acting from the belief that that they can essentially do whatever they want, and later deal with any consequences.

Imperialism applied in circumstances that lack the accompanying authority and power can be a dangerous undertaking. To the extent your imperial conduct conflicts with others who are unsympathetic to your desires, means, and circumstances, you may find that their lack of sympathy constrains and penalizes your ability to accomplish what you want. Those unsympathetic to imperial conduct may oppose what you want to do and how you want to do it. Further, if the imperial conduct crosses the line of certain ethical and legal standards, the attitude of ignoring the consequences may prove to be very expensive

To do what you want and ignore the consequences is a mistake.

167 Ask for Permission Later

Adherence to the *do-it-now* philosophy leads to the conclusion that it is better to get it done than to worry too much whether it is right.

Some companies adhere to the philosophy that it is better to ask for forgiveness later than to ask permission before, and not get it. The justification is that it is better to get it done and later worry about legal, ethical, customer, economic and strategic considerations. In some instances, but not always, it is better to put the primary emphasis on getting it done. But in some circumstances, failing to get permission can be precarious.

Ignoring getting permission can be a mistake.

168 Dealing with Problems after the Fact

Some companies favor dealing with problems after the fact.

The thinking behind a *dealing with problems after the fact* strategy is not to waste resources on a problem until it occurs. After all, maybe it won't occur, and then you won't need to do anything about it. This approach runs directly contrary to the adage that it is better to fix a leaky roof when the sun is shining than when it is raining. Sure, maybe it won't rain and therefore, you won't need to bother fixing the roof. But eventually, it will rain.

Dealing with problems after the fact is a mistake.

169 Violating Trust

Trust is one of the most important attributes you can have in any relationship.

The business and financial markets debacle of 2001 and 2002 is, at its core, all about violation of trust. Those companies who treated trust cavalierly, who made representations they did not honor, who made promises they did not fulfill, have suffered. Rebuilding their businesses will be difficult, for, once violated, trust is very hard to reestablish.

One of the biggest mistakes you can make is to violate trust.

170 Playing by the Rules

Many executives emphasize the importance of *playing by the rules*—not particularly laws and legal regulations but, the way things are done.

Paying attention to the way things are done—*playing by the rules*—can be important in some businesses because of the reliance on others for access to deal flow, industry gossip and the like. People *play by the rules* because they want this access and they want to get along at the country club. *Playing by the rules* is not for everyone. If you want to embark upon a contrary direction, to go your own way, to embrace differentiation, then *playing by the rules* is not the way to go.

To *play by the rules* can be a mistake.

171 Accountability Avoidance

Business involves accountability—the responsibility to one's self, to others and to the organization—to do what is agreed will be done.

Where accountability is lacking, where people chose not to accept and act upon their responsibilities, the chances of achieving the desired outcomes are much reduced. Companies populated by people who do not embrace accountability are much less likely to be successful than where accountability is present.

To avoid accountability is a mistake.

172 Disregarding the 80–20 Rule

There is a maxim in business that 80 percent of the results are produced by 20 percent of the people, resources, activities and so on.

The 80–20 rule and its variations—in some circumstances, the reality might be more 90–10 or even 95–5—have application to many facets of business. If you disregard the 80–20 rule, you may persist in spending more resources on less than productive activities. If, instead, you concentrated all of your resources on the most productive activities—and significantly reduced the resources spent on the least productive activities—you could dramatically improve the overall performance of your business.

To ignore the 80–20 rule can be a mistake.

173 Concentrating too Much on Problems

Because business involves many problems, there is a natural tendency to direct attention to problems.

While problems not addressed can be a major business liability, disproportionate attention and allocation of resources to problems can be equally as bad. Renowned management guru Peter Drucker has astutely observed that leaders should simply survive problems, and concentrate instead on opportunities. If excessive resources are devoted to problems, few resources will remain to address opportunities.

To devote disproportionate resources to problems at the expense of opportunities can be a mistake.

174 Reactive Rather Than Anticipatory in Dealing with Problems

Some people are proactive in dealing with problems, while others are reactive.

The reactive approach to problems is just that—reacting to a problem after it occurs. The proactive approach to problems, by contrast, involves anticipating the problem and dealing with it beforehand. This anticipatory approach may involve fewer resources to resolve the problem—or may actually prevent the problem from occurring.

To be reactive rather than anticipatory in dealing with problems can be a mistake.

175 Disproportionate Reliance upon a Scarlet O'Hara Philosophy

Scarlet O'Hara, the heroine of *Gone With The Wind,* addressed her problems with an "I'll think about that tomorrow" attitude.

It makes sense to worry about problems when they need to be worried about. Those who get a lot done in life do not spend disproportionate energies and concerns worrying about problems. They get on with things. But too much of an "I'll think about it tomorrow" attitude can be dangerous. For some situations, if tomorrow has not been anticipated and planned for, the consequences can be dire.

To rely too much on a Scarlet O'Hara "I'll think about that tomorrow" attitude can be a mistake.

176 Confusing Exploration with Exploitation

It is important to recognize that the function of exploration is very different than the function of exploitation.

Exploration can be thought of as searching for a new way, discovering a new opportunity, and finding something that has not been previously known. Exploitation, on the other hand, involves realizing the potential of this new discovery, opportunity, or way of doing things. Exploration involves innovation and creativity, while exploitation involves implementation and operations. Exploration and exploitation are very different and thereby require very different approaches, capabilities and mindsets.

Confusing exploration with exploitation can be a mistake.

177 Everything Is a Nail

It is said that if your tool is a hammer, then everything you encounter seems to be a nail.

If you have only one tool, the tendency is to use that tool universally in all situations, irrespective of the appropriateness of doing so. While in times past a single tool approach to business may have worked quite well, today problems and issues increasingly demand multiple tools in the toolkit.

To think of every problem as a nail can be a big mistake.

178 Too Much Acceptance of Failure

In recent times, a management idea emerged that people should be encouraged to take risks and fail.

As important as it is to encourage people to take risks, if there is not a concurrent emphasis on positive, successful outcomes, you may find that people are insufficiently prioritizing the imperative of successful outcomes. There also needs to be an emphasis on success, not just failure. If the organization is overly tolerant of failure, it can breed a failure-oriented culture. It is not enough just to take risks and fail. You also have to succeed some of the time; otherwise you have an organization that is dominated by failure.

It is a mistake to put so much emphasis on failure that you never get success.

179 Knowing When to Use Management Tools

The complexity of business today mandates managers having multiple tools in the managerial toolkit.

No longer is it workable to get by with just one management approach. The effective executive employs multiple management approaches. Consequently, managers are challenged to master multiple management tools. But just as important as having multiple tools is having the knowledge to know which tool to use in which situation—as well as the skill to use the tool in that situation.

If you do not know how and when to use the appropriate management tool, you may make a major mistake.

180 Insufficient Skill to Use Managerial Tools

As business has become ever more complex, the number of management tools and the skills required to operate those management tools has increased.

Anyone who owns a tool but does not know how to use that tool is at a fundamental disadvantage. If you lack the skill to use a tool, even though you possess the tool and you know the appropriate situation for using that tool, the effectiveness of that tool is decreased, to the point of your being not much different than the person who neither knows when to use a specific tool or doesn't even possess it.

Lacking the requisite skill to use important management tools is a mistake.

181 Lack of Commitment

Commitment is crucial to success in many endeavors. If commitment is lacking, the prospects of success are decreased.

Commitment is important to success in competitive endeavors, because of the imperative to be dedicated, persevering and steadfast in adhering to the agreed direction. Since conflict, difficulties and reversals are inevitable, commitment is crucial to surviving obstacles and realizing success. If you lack commitment to stay the course, you can rarely accomplish what you desire.

It is a mistake to pursue any important endeavor when commitment is lacking.

182 Ignoring How to Get the Result

If you ignore how to get the result, you seldom ever achieve it.

At least or as more important than a desired result is the consideration of how to get the result. If you just insist that people get a result, you may end up being frustrated or, worse, encouraging them to engage in wrongful conduct. While in certain circumstances it is appropriate to tell people what outcome is desired—and then let them figure out how best to get it—in other circumstances, it can be precarious to fail to consider the means by which the result is achieved. People may not be able to get the result you desire, or if they do get the desired result, the means they employ may compromise not only the result but larger level issues.

To ignore how to get the result can be a mistake.

183 Resource Mismatch

If your resources are not appropriately matched, you may be more likely to fail than to succeed.

If you have high-end equipment and tools for one part of an operation but much less sophisticated and less powerful tools and equipment for another part of an operation, you will not be nearly as effective as if your tools and equipment were congruent and compatible. If you want to get ahead, you employ matched and congruent resources, not mismatched and unbalanced resources.

A resource mismatch is a strategy mistake.

INDIVIDUAL STYLE

184 Too Close to the Decision

If you are too close to the decision, you may not make the most effective decision.

If you are too close to the decision, you may lack perspective that a more detached vantage point can bring. You may not only emphasize the bark at the expense of the trees, but you may also misperceive the forest. If you are too close to the decision, you may miss the bigger picture.

To be too close to the decision can be a mistake.

185 Too Much Management Involvement

Managers are challenged to balance how much to be involved in guiding, helping, and directing their workers in getting the work done.

If a manager provides too much direction and guidance, the workers will probably, especially if they wish to please the manager, do what the manager says. But that may not be the best way to do it. Too much management involvement may deny the manager the benefit of the workers' better way of doing it. And workers are denied the opportunity to express their own initiative and creativity.

Too much manager involvement can be a mistake.

186 Confusing Task Excellence with Managerial Competence

Task excellence is not the same thing as managerial competence.

Performing tasks and *managing* tasks are very different activities. The fact that an individual is an outstanding salesperson does not necessarily mean that individual would be an outstanding sales manager. Some managers who excel at performing a particular task are not particularly good at managing those tasks. Conversely, some managers who have only limited ability to perform a task may be highly effective in managing the performance of those tasks by others.

Confusing task excellence and managerial competence is a mistake.

187 Too Little Management Involvement

Some managers favor a "tell them what I want and let them figure out how to do it," style.

One idea behind a hands-off management style is to let the workers go about a task in the way they think best. In reality, some managers are hands-off because they are lazy, disinclined to do much of the heavy lifting, and would rather let others do the hard work. In such a circumstance, the ultimate quality of the work may suffer if the workers lack the constructive leadership, inspiration, and guidance that the manager could provide. To be too hands off can compromise the effectiveness of the work.

It can be a mistake for a manager to be too little involved.

188 The Issue Is Closed

Some people seek to put an end to a discussion by proclaiming, with finality, "the issue is closed."

While protracted discussion of a topic that does not justify a protracted discussion is inappropriate, so, too, is prematurely terminating a discussion. If you proclaim to another person, whose good will is important to you, that the issue is closed, you essentially are communicating to that person that you do not value their point of view, you do not value him or her and/or you do not value the relationship.

Prematurely and inappropriately proclaiming that the issue is closed can be one of the biggest mistakes you may make.

189 It Is Out of My Hands

Sometimes people in business will tell a customer or an employee that they cannot do something, saying, "it is out of my hands."

Stating "it is out of my hands" is basically stating that you do not care enough about the issue and the person involved to do something about it. "It is out of my hands" is another way of saying, "I don't' really care—it is not important—you are not important." Someone who cares takes the initiative to find a solution, to find the person who can solve the problem, and then advocates getting the right outcome. It is much better to say, "I can take care of it," than to say, "it is out of my hands."

To say, "it is out of my hands" is a mistake.

190 I'm Sorry, but That's Our Policy

Rather than figuring out how to solve a problem, some managers abdicate their responsibility and then justify that abdication by proclaiming "I'm sorry, but that's our policy."

Policies are important in business, for they can achieve consistent treatment of others, streamline decision making, and improve overall effectiveness. But policies should not be rigidly and inflexibly applied to the point that they dominate and ultimately destroy customer relationships. Saying "I'm sorry but that's our policy" is saying that the individual situation, the individual's concerns, and the individual are less important than the policy.

The effective manager does what's right, not merely what's policy. If an approval for a policy exception is needed, then the effective manager gets it. The effective manager does not damage or destroy a relationship merely to comply with the policy.

To rigidly stick by "I'm sorry, but that's our policy" is a mistake.

191 Too Busy to Have Time for Anyone Who Is Not Important

Some executives are so busy that they just do not have time for anyone who is not important.

To be a senior executive today can be very daunting, for there are extraordinary demands on time, attention and resources—demands which collectively exceed the available supply of time. One way some senior executives cope with these demands is to be highly discriminating in how they allocate their time. One discrimination standard that certain executives may employ is not to spend anytime with people that they do not perceive to be important. The problem with this strategy is that the executive may misperceive who is really important. Somebody who is apparently unimportant today may be very important tomorrow. Someone who the executive thinks is important, may, in fact, be relatively unimportant.

To be too busy to have time for people who are not important can be a very expensive mistake.

192 Disrespecting the Receptionist

Some people are so self-absorbed that they cannot be bothered to show much respect for others who they do not perceive as necessarily helping them get what they want.

Once an individual was at the final interview stage for a highly coveted position. This particular individual was told to arrive at the company headquarters at 9 a.m. for his final interview. When he arrived, the receptionist informed him that the schedule was running a little bit late and asked would he mind waiting. Periodically, the receptionist informed the individual that it was still not quite time. When the receptionist tried to engage the individual in some polite conversation, he responded rudely and rebuffed her overtures to engage in conversation.

Eventually, the receptionist informed the individual that it was time to go in for the meeting. The interview turned out to be much shorter than the individual expected. What the job applicant did not comprehend was that the receptionist was part of the interview panel. Before the job applicant got to the interview, he had already been rejected from consideration.

Being disrespectful to the receptionist may be a very important mistake.

193 Micro Managing

Some hands-on managers insist on having their hands on everything.

While some workers need and others appreciate lots of supervisor involvement in their work, in other circumstances it can be counter-productive. If a manager is too involved in looking over the shoulder of the workers—to the point of interfering in their work or frustrating them—the result can be quite disappointing. Too much micro-management can both compromise people doing the work and also distract resources from more important managerial tasks.

Too much micro-management is a mistake.

194 Talking about the Importance of Team but Acting Like the Lone Ranger

Many executives go to great lengths to talk about the importance of a team approach.

Many executives put a lot of emphasis on people in their organization being team players. Perhaps they encountered the idea in a management textbook or maybe an organizational consultant told them it would be a good thing to do. But talk is one thing, and action is another. An executive who talks about the importance of team and how he expects everyone to be a team player, but if he himself is not a team player, may find that over time he does not have much of a team to play on.

Talking about the team but not being a team player can be a mistake.

195 Employing only One Communication Style

The most effective executives adapt their communication style to circumstances, people and place.

But the communication style you favor may not be the communication style that the audience favors. If the desired result is important to you, you will address what the audience needs and wants, rather than just what you need and want. You will elect the communication style favored by the audience.

Peter Drucker once profoundly observed that it is crucial to success in business to understand how people with whom you interact want to receive information, and then to present the information to them in that form. Applying Peter Drucker's wisdom, it is important to understand whether people want to receive information: (1) verbally, in writing, or a combination—and in which sequence; (2) in an outline, PowerPoint format, or narrative text; (3) with the conclusion stated first and then the rationale provided, or the conclusion presented at the end; (4) through a short or lengthy presentation; or (5) in an inductive or deductive argument style. By being adaptive to the audience, you have a much better likelihood of achieving the desired outcome.

Employing your favored communication style without considering your audience's preferences can be a mistake.

196 Fiefdom Primacy

Many executives are much more concerned with how their own fiefdom performs than how the overall corporation performs.

In medieval days, the fiefdom was the primary focus of organizational concern. While fiefdom primacy may have been workable in some settings in medieval times, those corporations that allow fiefdom primacy at the expense of the corporations' overall outcomes and results do so at their peril. While it is important for business units to be self-contained in promoting their own activities, to lose sight of the larger whole and larger purposes is unacceptable.

Fiefdom primacy is a mistake.

197 Saying One Thing but Doing Another

Some people in business will say one thing but do another.

Some executives proclaim the importance of people. These executives assert that their primary concern is for employees, customers and shareholders. Yet when it comes to critical decisions that these executives make, it is evident by their actions—which of course, speak louder than their words—that they promote their own individual interests over those of the company, its shareholders, customers, employees and other stakeholders. Statements these executives make about what is important are contradicted by what they do.

To say one thing and do another is a mistake.

198 Leaders Who Fail to Learn from Their Reports

Learning theory scholars know that learning is not a one-way transmission of information, but a two-way transmission.

The most effective teachers learn from their students at the same time that they teach their students. Indeed, brilliant instructors enjoy being in the classroom because of what they learn, not just for the satisfaction of imparting what they know to their students. Learning is not a one-way, but rather a two-way street. Executives who fail to learn from their colleagues—especially those who report to them—are much less effective than those that do.

Executives who to fail to learn from their colleagues are making a mistake.

199 Leaders Who Cannot Look in the Mirror Cannot See What Is in the Mirror

Some people are in perpetual interpersonal denial—being unable to recognize how their own behavior compromises their enterprise's effectiveness.

Even though a leader may receive continual inputs about the dysfunctionality of certain behavior—for example, failing to treat people with respect, failing to share information or rewards, focusing on short-term results at the expense of long-term outcomes, or sacrificing people to achieve a personal priority—these leaders may persist in perpetuating this behavior. Even though they are confronted with an organizational mirror, by virtue of having been told the same thing over and over by many people, they do not hear it. Such denial as to how they interact with and treat their people can have significant adverse consequences for the organization.

Leaders who cannot look in the mirror may make a mistake.

200 Failing to Listen to what People Have to Say

The critically important communications element of management is a multi-part process, involving both conveying messages and *receiving* messages.

To receive a message, you need to *listen.* If an executive is not able to genuinely listen to what his people have to say, that executive may be denied access to significant information that could have a major impact upon the company's success. It is not enough for the executive to profess to listen. To genuinely listen is what is important.

Company managers who lack the capacity to genuinely listen to customers and employees may make a mistake.

201 Engaging in "Faux Listening" and Not Really Acting Upon What You Hear

Some people have a pattern of "listening" to what other people have to say, but then proceeding as if they never heard what was said.

On one level, listening at all is better than not listening. But on a deeper, more important level, if you listen and do not hear—if you go through the motions of listening but do not act upon what you hear, if you do not face up to what you are told and do something about it—such so-called listening does nothing more than setting up a sham of caring without any follow-through of action. Such a style inherently compromises the company's productivity. Companies that tolerate such behavior compromise their ability to achieve what they otherwise would.

To listen but to not really hear is a mistake.

202 Not Getting Out of the Office

Some executives associate doing business with being in the office.

While much of business takes place in the office, some of the most important business takes place out of the office. Many customer interactions most advantageously occur out of the office. Market intelligence, supplier due diligence, and certain recruiting interactions may be most effectively done outside of the office. Certain critical employee meetings are much more productive if conducted outside of the office. If the company's executives never venture outside of the office, their perspectives, information access, and opportunities are limited.

To never get outside of the office is a mistake.

203 Competitive Blindness

Some companies are blind to the reality that they are in competition.

Although some executives may not recognize it, companies are in competition for every resource that they wish to employ in their business. Companies compete for customer accounts, customer budgets, supplier relationships, preferred supplier attention, employees, employees' energy and attention, capital, shareholders' contributions, community support and more. Companies that are successful prevail in the many competitions for resources, attention, and loyalty. Companies that are blind to the reality that they are in competition for critical resources inevitably fall short of being what they might otherwise be.

Competitive blindness is a mistake.

204 Too Busy To Get Out of the Office

Some executives work so hard that they never have time to get out of the office.

Executives hard at work in the company may decide that they simply cannot afford to go to an industry meeting, to attend a professional development program, or to shop the competition. They're too busy doing what they're doing to do anything else. As a consequence, they have less knowledge, less capability, fewer perspectives and fewer fresh ideas than if they get out of the office. Such executives are at a disadvantage to those who do get out of the office and thereby get access to new thinking and new ideas.

It is a mistake to be so busy that you can never get out of the office.

205 Relying Only on Traditional Sources of Information

Most executives follow very conventional, structured sources of gaining access to information.

There is a saying that you are what you read. If you read the same thing, week after week, month after month, year after year, your thinking will not be likely to change. If you are not challenged with new ideas, new concepts, and new approaches, you are unlikely to be in a position to identify, anticipate the consequences of, and respond to change. By implementing a conscious strategy of gaining access to disparate, eclectic and unconventional information sources, you increase your likelihood of being more insightful as to what is truly going on.

Relying only upon conventional information sources is a mistake.

206 Reading Only Industry Magazines

Many managers make a point of reading industry magazines.

Managers read industry magazines in order to know what is going on in business and in their markets, to interact with competitors, to discover new practices and technologies, and to identify trends that may impact their company's strategy. But if managers limit their reading to standard industry publications, they are less likely to be exposed to ideas that counter traditional industry thinking.

Ian Schrager, who co-created the famed Studio 54 nightclub in Manhattan and pioneered the hip boutique hotel, makes a point of reading up to 50 different magazines in every conceivable field. Marketing guru Dan Kennedy periodically will buy 30 or 40 eclectic magazines on topics that he does not regularly read to find out what new is happening. One reason that Schrager, Kennedy and other leading executives are creative is that they don't limit their magazines to the traditional industry publications.

Limiting your magazine reading to traditional industry publications can be a mistake.

COMPETITION AND MARKETS

207 One-Trick Pony

Some businesses employ the same format to deal with every issue or problem that comes along.

Employing the same format to deal with every issue or problem that comes along is akin to having a one-trick pony. The one-trick pony has just one trick. If you're satisfied with just one trick, then the one-trick pony is all you need for a great show. But if you want more, if you want some diversity, if you want the capability to respond to different situations, then you are out of luck if the one-trick pony is all that you have. Employing the same format to solve all problems and to address all issues can limit the business's capabilities to achieve all of the success that it could with more flexible capabilities.

To rely on a one-trick pony can be a mistake.

208 Competitive Naïveté

Some companies are naïve about competition.

The role of competition can vary across places, time, settings, circumstances, industries and cycles. Some businesses are highly competitive all of the time, and others may seem to have very little competition. But just because the business has not previously faced competitive challenge, that does not mean that it may not encounter significant competitive challenges in the future. To ignore the reality of competition is naïve—and ultimately dangerous.

Competitive naïveté is a mistake.

209 Running a Long-term Event as Contrasted to a Business

Companies that occupy a prime business space, which business space is crucial to their customer relationships, may find, if they're not careful, that they are really running a long-term event, as contrasted to an ongoing business with a viable, controllable future.

A business has continuity as a consequence of customer relationships, and the ability to interact with those customers on an ongoing basis. If the company only has contact with its customers when the customers choose to come into their retail facility, and the retail facility is leased from a third party, the company really has a long-term event—profitable as long as the company continues to occupy that space, but with limited capacity to transfer the customer relationships to another location. If your business is tied primarily to a customer coming to a single location, which you do not control over the long term, you really do not have a business for the long term—what you have is a long-term event, whose value depends on your being able to stay at a location that is controlled by others.

To pursue a long-term event as opposed to having a real business is a mistake.

210 Relying on the Lottery Approach

Too many companies take a lottery approach to business.

The lottery approach to business involves hoping something good will happen, but having no real plan to make it happen. The lottery approach is characterized by someone who buys a lottery ticket, knowing either consciously or unconsciously that the odds are against them, but somehow, someway, hoping that their lucky number will come up. Against all odds they hope that they will be rewarded with a fortune. The lottery approach to a job means putting up with work that you don't like, in the hope that somehow, some way things will change for the better. The lottery approach to business means leaving things to chance, as contrasted to having a plan, taking responsibility and initiating the work that is necessary to get the results you want.

Relying on a lottery approach to business, hoping something good will happen but having no plan to make it happen, is a mistake.

211 Not Bothering With the Fundamentals

Some people are so involved in creative approaches and applications that they can't be bothered with fundamentals.

Although you may get by with ignoring fundamentals for a while, eventually, ignoring fundamentals will catch up with you. Every great athlete and every great coach emphasizes the importance of fundamentals. Without attention to fundamentals, you have no foundation to build upon. If you want to achieve true excellence, you emphasize fundamentals.

Ignoring fundamentals is a mistake.

212 Failing to Monitor Your Competition

Because business is a competitive undertaking, it is crucial to understand the competition.

If a company and its leaders fail to monitor the competition, the company will not know what the competition is up to. If you do not know what the competition is up to, then how can you compete with them effectively? Competitive intelligence is central to superior business outcomes. By operating in a vacuum, without insight into what the competition is doing, the company will be less successful than if it had access to knowledge of what the competition is doing.

To fail to monitor the competition is a mistake.

213 Being in a Business Competing with Microsoft

Business success ultimately is a function of how you relate to the competition.

If you compete with very aggressive, powerful, ruthless, resource-rich competitors, your prospects for success are much less than if your competition were neither so daunting nor so intimidating. If you compete with Microsoft, you must be aware that Microsoft does not tolerate competitors. Microsoft's management mantra is domination and destruction of competitors. Microsoft expects to monopolize any market in which it offers products. If you choose to compete with Microsoft on its terms, you will likely be acquired or annihilated. To have the best prospects for prevailing in competition with Microsoft, you should compete on your terms, not their terms. Competing successfully with Microsoft requires pursuing a strategy that does not visibly or directly challenge the company's massive installed base and its insistence on monopolizing its markets.

To compete with a market-monopolist such as Microsoft on their terms can be a mistake.

214 Thinking the Competitor Lacks Intestinal Fortitude

Some companies proceed in reliance on the belief that their competitors lack the intestinal fortitude to undertake a particular business activity or strategic direction.

If you rely on the assumption that a competitor lacks intestinal fortitude, you may find that you're mistaken. If the competitor actually does have the courage to do whatever you presume the competitor would not do, and if you presume that a certain action, initiative or new direction is, for some reason, out of bounds for the competitor to consider, you may find that the competitor surprises you and does what you think that they will not do. If you think the competitor lacks intestinal fortitude—a willingness to undertake whatever difficulty or hardship that may be required to get to a desired end—you may find that the competitor surprises you.

Presuming your competitor lacks intestinal fortitude can be a big mistake.

215 Unwilling to Consider the Competitor's Technology

Increasingly, today, companies are employing technology from whatever source offers the best technology—even if that source is a competitor.

Unwillingness to consider technology from non-traditional sources, such as from competitors, can constrain a company's capabilities. If a company is unwilling to consider technology other than its own, its competitive position may erode. A company unwilling to consider alternative sources for technology—even if those alternative sources are its competitors—may be less successful than those companies which are not constrained in doing whatever it takes to get access to the best technology.

Unwillingness to consider alternative technology sources, including accessing competitor's technology, can be a mistake.

216 Obeying Industry Norms

Every industry has norms—a certain standard way things are done.

Professional associations, various companies, and some people—with perhaps too much time on their hands—may call you to task if you do something that violates industry norms. Because these people choose to comply with the norms of the industry, they insist that you should comply. Complying with industry norms may not always be the best business decision and in fact may sometimes be a recipe for mediocrity. Violating industry norms may be the path to distinction and outstanding outcomes.

To always adhere to industry norms may be a mistake.

217 Competitive Arrogance

Some companies are arrogant in the extreme.

While a high degree of confidence goes with the territory of success, too much confidence that becomes arrogance can be disastrous. Arrogance can blind companies to competitive threats, lead to self-satisfaction, and result in susceptibility to being outsmarted, outhustled, and outperformed. The arrogant company does not understand that each day it must compete for and earn the respect, interest and involvements of those whose allegiance it needs. To think that other companies are not competing for the same thing is arrogant—and ultimately dangerous.

Competitive arrogance is a mistake.

218 Lowest Common Denominator

In seeking to be agreeable and to accommodate many people, some companies may choose a *lowest common denominator* approach.

The *lowest common denominator* means you accommodate the least able, least sophisticated, least demanding supplier, customer or employee. Although being accommodating may be a desirable thing to do, if being accommodating means that you default to a *lowest common denominator* approach, you may be losing out—on the best suppliers, the best customers, the best employees.

To adopt the *lowest common denominator* approach can be a mistake.

219 Don't Rock the Boat

Many businesses follow the *don't rock the boat* rule, meaning that they do not wish to do anything that would disrupt the way things are now being done.

While in certain instances a *don't rock the boat* approach is called for, in other instances *don't rock the boat* can be a recipe for less than superior outcomes. If you have a *don't rock the boat* attitude, then necessarily you stay clear of swift moving streams and currents, which are the very conditions that can lead to accelerated progress and superior outcomes.

If you want to get ahead, you may find that *don't rock the boat* is a mistake.

220 Unconstrained *Chutzpah* in Public Settings

Organizations that have both high visibility and a high level of public accountability necessarily are held to higher standards than may apply to other organizations.

Enterprises with a high profile must recognize that their very visibility imposes limitations on conduct, since their conduct might be more critically scrutinized than in an organization with a lower profile. In the instance of an organization with a public responsibility, the level of scrutiny can be especially pronounced Consequently, behavior that might pass without comment or concern in one setting, could, for a high-visibility enterprise with a public responsibility, be considered to be not just inappropriate but to represent unrestrained *chutzpah*. Unrestrained *chutzpah* in the wrong circumstances can have very significant consequences.

Engaging in unrestrained *chutzpah* can be a mistake.

221 Monkey See, Monkey Do

Too many businesses operate on a *monkey see, monkey* do basis.

Monkey see, monkey do means that what the company does is what it observes. Merely because the company observes other monkeys doing something, that does not mean that its monkeys should do the same thing. Many companies perpetrate approaches that reflect the antithesis of enlightenment. Why? Because others do the same thing.

Monkey see, monkey do is a mistake.

222 Quick Fix

In the contemporary fast-paced, do-it-now business environment, many companies are disinclined to consider a problem resolution approach. They want results now. They want the quick fix. They want prompt resolution.

If you can get it done faster rather than slower, everything else being equal, faster is generally better. But if faster means compromising quality and increasing longer term risk, faster may not be the best approach. A quick fix may not be the best way to go.

Sometimes a quick fix is a mistake.

223 Disregarding the Out-of-the-Box Solution

When companies need to embark upon a new system or procedure, the choice is a variant on the classic make-or-buy decision: do you favor a customization route or do you seek an existing product or solution that can provide the desired functionality?

Although customization may ultimately be the preferred approach to meet a desired need, customization is not always the best way to go. Customization can involve greater complexity, take more time, use up more resources, and incur more out-of-pocket costs. Oftentimes, choosing the existing, established solution can be the more cost-effective approach. By reducing the need for customization, the payoff can be sooner and less expensive.

To rely solely on customization to meet new systems needs can be a mistake.

224 Disregarding the Customization Approach

It has been accurately said that much of business involves a series of make-or-buy decisions. The choice is whether you buy what already exists or make something new.

The buy approach, of course, involves buying the existing product or solution that provides the desired functionality. The make solution, on the other hand, involves more initiative, creativity and risk. Often the make solution is more expensive than the buy solution. Consequently, certain factors may favor buying the out-of-the-box solution rather than the customization approach. But in some circumstances, customization is the better way to go.

Disregarding the customization approach can be a mistake.

225 No Preparation to Exploit the Big Chance

When you get the big chance, you had better be prepared to exploit it, or you may find that your opportunity has come and gone.

To exploit the big chance, you need to be appropriately prepared. Consider the author who had coveted an opportunity to be on the Oprah Winfrey show. Finally, this author was invited to appear on the show. However, the author had no preparation in place to exploit this opportunity. He had no additional products and services ready to offer, nor did he have the organizational infrastructure in place to respond to leads or to serve all of the inquiries. The author was not really able to derive the full potential benefit from his big chance.

If you do not prepare to be ready to exploit the big chance, you may find you have made a very expensive mistake.

226 Failing to Do Due Diligence

Fundamental to any major capital commitment is due diligence.

Due diligence involves the investigations that a prudent person would undertake before committing substantial capital to an enterprise characterized by risk. Due diligence is done before a major investment, a major corporate transaction, or a major capital commitment. If you fail to do due diligence, the commitment you make may be a mistake. This is what happened to renowned former GE CEO Jack Welsh, when he promoted a merger with Honeywell, only to find that the European anti-trust regulations precluded the transaction. As he ruefully admitted, he and GE failed to do the requisite due diligence.

Failing to do due diligence is a mistake.

227 Failure To Initiate Problem Identification

Some business philosophers say that business is all about solving problems.

The measure of an executive is the capacity of that executive to solve problems. But if the problem is not identified, it cannot be solved. Companies that fail to have a culture and climate that identifies problems—in advance of when they might occur—will inevitably suffer disappointing financial performance. By contrast, companies that have the capacity to initiate effective problem identification can perform at a much higher level than those that do not.

If you fail to initiate problem identification you may make a mistake.

228 Failure To Initiate Effective Problem Resolution

Problems are inevitable in business.

A company whose management team can effectively resolve problems has a major edge over competitors who lack that skill. Too often, problem solutions reflect a lack of imagination, common sense, systems thinking, and thoroughness. If a company is ineffective in solving problems, it inevitably is an ineffective company.

Failure to initiate effective problem solution is a big mistake.

229 Blinded by Success

Some have the attitude that if you achieve success, nothing else really matters.

One of the consequences of a total commitment to success is that other issues, considerations, and concerns may be downplayed or even ignored. If those other issues and concerns are not appropriately addressed, the team and capabilities that achieved the earlier success may not be able to repeat that success. If the success blinds considerations to other issues, the prospects of replicating that success may be compromised.

To be blinded by your own success can be a mistake.

230 Buying a Solution as Contrasted to Doing it Yourself

Many companies, when confronted with a problem, figure that they can buy a solution.

Buying a solution is appealing, for the idea is that if you just pay some company enough money, then they will take care of the problem for you. But buying a solution may be very shortsighted. True, lasting solutions to problems come from doing it yourself, by taking stock of the problem, figuring out what needs to be done; and then doing it. Certainly, you may buy a variety of resources to help you get to the solution, but ultimately, you must do it yourself.

To think that you can buy a wholesale solution without taking responsibility is a mistake.

231 Do-it-yourself

American cultural values emphasize self-reliance. Those who place a priority emphasis on self-reliance tend to be disinclined to ask for assistance.

The self-reliant manager is much more inclined to favor a do-it-yourself solution to a problem than to buy a solution from an expert. While in some instances a do-it-yourself approach is called for, relying on do-it-yourself may not be the best course, especially when third party expertise and resources can lead to a better result. A do-it-yourself approach can lead to a negative outcome, which could have been avoided by buying a solution from a competent, capable expert.

Inappropriate reliance on a do-it-yourself approach can be a mistake.

232 Counting on the Courts to Make It Right

If companies are disappointed in the marketplace or conclude that perhaps some expected outcome has failed to be realized, they may rely on the court to make it right.

Sometimes, courts can be a very effective avenue for achieving the results you expected to achieve in the marketplace—but did not. But not always. Courts can be capricious. Courts may reject overwhelmingly persuasive cases and accept weak, unsubstantiated, illogical arguments.

If you believe the courts will necessarily make it right, you may be mistaken.

233 Disregarding the Paper Trail

If you do not maintain appropriate records of decisions, policies, procedures, processes, and key relationships—relying, instead, on the "keeping everything in your head" approach—you may be at a big disadvantage.

Corporate memory can be an important business resource. Indeed, some people are especially valued because of the corporate memory and knowledge that they possess. However, corporate memory does not need to and should not be lodged only in the heads of certain individuals. Better for corporate memory to be committed to paper. If a company does not keep good records, then the ability to access critical, need-to-know information can be compromised, if those who keep everything in their heads are inaccessible or unavailable.

Failing to maintain a paper trail can be a mistake.

PERSPECTIVE AND VIEWPOINTS

234 Believing Success Yesterday Means Success Tomorrow

Many have the belief that the past is the best predictor of the future, which leads them to believe that success yesterday means success tomorrow.

Lacking any other source of information, a prior event is the best predictor of a future event. However, in the majority of instances and circumstances, tomorrow's factors differ from yesterday's factors. Tomorrow is not the same as yesterday. And if tomorrow is different from yesterday, then what it takes to be successful tomorrow will be different from what it took to be successful yesterday. If you did what achieved success yesterday, you may not necessarily be successful tomorrow. More than a few companies and individuals have learned this lesson—and continue to learn it.

To think that what made you successful yesterday will make you successful tomorrow is a mistake.

235 Obsession with the Past

Knowing the history and heritage of an industry, its markets, and the company itself, can all be very helpful in making more informed business decisions.

As important as it is to learn from the past, if you're too dominated by the past, you may find that your ability to move forward in the present and to capture future opportunities is constrained. If you're always looking backward, it is hard to look forward. Although the past is very important, you are living today in the present and tomorrow in the future. Understandably, people and organizations are influenced and formed by their prior experiences, but to spend too much time concerned with the past, at the expense of thinking about the future, is a miscalculation. Because the future will, in many ways, and varying degrees, diverge from the past, it is important in business to maintain a future focus.

To be overly concerned with the past is a mistake.

236 Not Taking the Opportunity to Learn from the Past

The philosopher Santana wisely counseled that those who ignore the lessons of the past are doomed to repeat the mistakes in the future. But obsession with the past can be a mistake.

From business history one can learn illuminating lessons that can guide future decisions. Certainly, the lessons of the past need to be adapted and adjusted to the circumstances of the present. But often, the very thinking process that was employed by others in making prior decisions, can be illuminating in determining how to deal with present decisions.

To ignore the opportunity to learn from the past can be a mistake.

237 No Sense of History

Some companies operate with an apparent benign innocence when it comes to history.

If your company lacks a sense of history, it lacks a sense of heritage, continuity, tradition, and carrying on of what has gone before. A company that lacks a sense of history has no roots, no anchor, and no foundation. Consequently, decisions that might responsibly be informed by a sense of history are made lacking a sense of history. And such decisions are often not as effective, responsive, or responsible as they might be, if they were made with the perspective of a sense of history.

To operate a business without a sense of history may be a mistake.

238 Managing Through the Rear View Mirror

It has been said that too many people in business are driving into the future with their eyes firmly fixed upon the rear view mirror.

Many of the business books that managers look to for guidance are more concerned about chronicling what has been, than addressing what might be. These books, which describe what worked in the past, may offer illuminating, even invaluable, lessons. But the essence of leadership is to consider what the future might be, in order to address the implications of new and different technologies, cultural priorities, and even world orders.

To look too much to the past and fail to address the future can be a mistake.

239 Pursuing a New Venture Incongruent with the Company's Heritage

When a company embarks upon a new venture, there is a fundamental question as to the connection between that new venture and the company's past.

If a new venture is essentially a line extension of a company's prior activities, then congruence and consistency with what has been done previously is especially important. A substantial investment management firm, known for its sophisticated quantitative approach to managing stocks and bonds, decided to add real estate investments to its product line. There were compelling reasons favoring such an initiative. The company chose a very unsophisticated style—which was the antithesis of how they managed stocks and bonds—for their real estate product. The fundamental incongruence between the legacy of the company and its new venture contributed to the lack of success in the new investment management activity.

To pursue a new venture that lacks consistency and congruency with the company's heritage can be a mistake.

240 Ignoring the Lessons of Extraordinarily Popular Delusions and the Madness of Crowds

Too many executives ignore the lessons of history.

A book that should be on the reading list of every executive is Charles MacKay's *Extraordinary Popular Delusions and the Madness of Crowds.* This classic volume, published in 1841, chronicles stories of financial miscalculations and violations of fiscal integrity, aided and abetted by delusionary thinking and crowd behavior. Of course, there have been recent installments to the story. Among these recent installments are Enron, some of the telecommunications companies, and many dot.com venture deals.

To ignore the lessons of *Extraordinary Popular Delusions and Madness of Crowds* can be a mistake.

241 Lack of Sense of Urgency

As a general proposition, things in life only happen when they are made to happen.

People who operate with a sense of urgency tend to get more done than those who adopt a more lackadaisical, relaxed style. When an important new initiative, a major transaction, or a critical priority must be addressed, a sense of urgency can support achieving a desired outcome. If urgency is lacking, the outcome may be delayed and less significant, than were a sense of urgency present.

Some of the most effective businesses are characterized by an acute sense of urgency. If your business lacks urgency, you may not get nearly as much done as a business where urgency is a watchword. Urgency can energize a company, motivating people to do more than they would normally otherwise do. Urgency can impress customers. If a company delivers results in time frames that competitors do not, urgency can be a path to profits and prosperity. If urgency is lacking, the company may not be nearly as successful as were if urgency were a priority.

Lack of sense of urgency can be a mistake.

242 Too Much Mañana

Some companies are disinclined to deal with issues or problems today, preferring to deal with them tomorrow.

If the company has a mañana approach to what it does and how it does it, the company may miss out on doing today what is needed to be done to be prepared for tomorrow. The company may be so oriented to mañana that it does not take care of business today.

Too much mañana may be a mistake.

243 Never Been Done Before

Some companies emphasize doing only what they have done before.

When presented with an interesting, innovative idea, the company that emphasizes doing only that which was done before, may reject that idea, as appealing as it might be. If the company emphasizes only doing what it has done before, then it cannot consider doing new things. To the extent customer preference, competitor initiatives, or market conditions change, the company may be highly vulnerable. But, of course, the company can't consider doing anything else, because it will only consider what it has done before.

To consider only doing what you have done before is a big mistake.

244 Short-term Interim Permanence Orientation

Some enterprises seem to be more interim or short-term in their orientation than permanent.

If your company lacks a sense of permanence, your customers may not be inclined to make the commitments that they would make to a company that they perceive has a sense of permanence. Without a sense of permanence, employees may be disinclined to make the commitments that they would, if you had a sense of permanence. Lacking a sense of permanence, business decisions may be guided more by short-term considerations than what may be best for the company over the longer term, and the company may not realize the outcomes that could be realized if it had a sense of permanence.

To employ more of a short-term interim orientation than a sense of permanence can be a mistake.

245 Excessive Emphasis on the Short Term

Because business moves at such a fast pace these days, many managers are drawn to emphasize the short term.

The emphasis on the short term is understandable, for 24-hour news, 15 minutes of fame and sound-bite journalism all conspire to downplay the long term and emphasize the short term. In an accelerated, fast-paced business environment, it is natural that companies are pointed towards the short term. As important as the short term is, if the company puts too much emphasis on the short term, it may find that its business performance suffers. But too much emphasis on the short term can be dangerous if more important long-term priorities are either ignored or overtly sacrificed. Rather than focusing predominantly on the short term, it would be better to have a more balanced approach to its business time horizons.

To place too much emphasis on the short term can be a mistake.

246 Too Much Emphasis on the Long Term

Because many business issues take a considerable period of time to play out, certain companies may take a very long-term orientation to their basic decisions.

As important as the long term is, if excessive emphasis is placed upon the long term, a company may find that intermediate and short-term issues are short-changed. Too much emphasis on the long term can deflect needed attention from interim issues, tasks, decisions and actions that must be competently, responsibly, and effectively implemented in order to achieve long-term objectives.

Too much emphasis on the long term can be a mistake.

247 Pay Me Now or Pay Me Later

A classic advertisement for an automobile maintenance company pronounced that drivers had a *pay me now or pay me later* choice. Drivers could either get the maintenance they needed now or pay much more later, because maintenance not done on a current basis would be much more expensive later.

Companies that put off until later what should be done now, may find that it is much more expensive to deal with the problems later on. As painful as it may be, generally *pay me now* is a better proposition than *pay me later.* Not only is the *pay me late*r approach more expensive, but it is disadvantageous because the need to correct something that is deferred may come up without warning, and thereby be more disruptive than would be a managed *pay me now* approach. Further, if resources that should be spent currently are not spent, the company may gain a false sense of prosperity, presuming it is really doing better than it actually is. Then, when the greater amount of resources are needed to be spent, *the pay me later* solution will be more expensive, not just in cash payments but in performance reporting and the confidence of external investors and management.

Pay me later is a mistake.

248 Pay for It Later Mentality

Some companies approach liabilities with a *pay for it later* mentality—as contrasted to a *pay for it now* mentality.

Pay for it later mentality involves applying the American consumer attitude of instant-gratification and defer-the-consequences to major business decisions, as contrasted to the approach of deferring buying until you can afford to pay for it. The problem with *pay for it later* is that there may be a mismatch between the company's productive resources and the claim on those resources. The company may find that some part of its current productivity must be applied to paying for the past.

Pay for it later can be a mistake.

249 Moving So Fast There Is No Time to Reflect

Many businesses advocate moving fast.

In the 21st century, if you do not move fast, you may get left behind. But if you move too fast, you may have no time for reflection. If you do not reflect, you may miss things, you may miscalculate, you may misjudge.

To move so fast that there is no time to reflect can be a mistake.

250 Resistance to Change

Some organizations resist change—and are committed to doing things in the ways they have always done them.

Resistance to change can compromise a company's performance. A company that resists change is unwilling to explore new ways of doing things, to consider new opportunities, or to embark upon new directions. Resistance to change can mire a company in what was, rather than what might be.

Resistance to change can be a mistake.

251 Change for Change's Sake

Some companies are so desirous of being hip and cool that they embrace any change that comes along. These companies change for change's sake—without considering whether the change is appropriate, justified or worthwhile.

Change for change's sake can be pernicious. Change for change's sake destroys any sense of continuity, and frustrates people who expect that tomorrow will be an extension of today and yesterday. Change for change's sake can lead to inefficiency, ineffectiveness and performance shortfall.

Change for change's sake can be a mistake.

252 Believing That Change Must Be All or Nothing

Some change advocates believe that change must be done on an overall, comprehensive basis—or not at all.

Although some circumstances may call out for massive, comprehensive, extraordinary change, that is not always the best approach. While in some companies, change is best done on an overall basis, in others it is best done piece by piece. In some circumstances, change should be implemented from the bottom up, rather from the top down. It is important that a change program be customized to the company, rather than rigidly imposed on an overall basis.

To think that change must be an all or nothing proposition is a mistake.

253 Rejecting Deviant Thinking

Some executives reject deviant thinking—and by so doing may make a mistake.

Deviant thinking, by definition, deviates from accepted, established norms. Deviant thinking may be uncomfortable, unpleasant or challenging to established practice, and difficult to integrate with the way things are generally done. Because much of business is premised upon structured processes, disciplined routines, and automation, deviation is a contradiction to the established ways of doing things. But if you reject deviant thinking, you may reject the payoff that may be realized from deviant thinking.

To reject deviant thinking can be a mistake.

254 Rejecting a Big Idea Because of Misinterpretation of a Component Part

If a component part of an idea is misinterpreted, some may be tempted to reject the larger idea.

In evaluating a big idea, it is important to base the evaluation on the fullness and totality of the idea, rather than upon an assessment of a component part. All too often, a big idea is rejected on the basis of a dubious application of a component part of an idea. In assessing big ideas, it is important to base the evaluation on the big idea itself, not on a component part.

If you reject a big idea because of a deficiency in the interpretation or application of a component part, you may be making a big mistake.

255 Placing More Emphasis on Where an Idea Comes From

In deciding which ideas to implement in business, some people place their primary emphasis on where the idea comes from.

Because change challenges the familiar, it is understandable that in coping with change, many seek an anchor in familiarity. The anchor of familiarity in the face of change favors ideas that originate from a familiar source. But a familiar source may not have a monopoly on the best ideas. Enterprises that achieve true distinction recognize that not all of the best ideas come from a familiar source.

To favor an idea from a familiar source over the idea that is best for the company can be a mistake.

256 Believing That Robust Expansion Is the Best Time to Start or Expand a Business

In good times, many people are attracted either to start a new venture or to expand an existing one.

The thinking behind expanding a business in good times is that the basic momentum of the flow will carry you along. Yes, it is true, in positive economic times the marketplace is more receptive. But there are downsides to building a business in good times. Because talented people are harder to come by when demand is strong, your cost structure may be higher than appropriate. With so much activity, it is much harder to stand out and differentiate yourself. And you may find that you have built a business that really is justified only by good times momentum, not by fundamental rationale. When bad times come along, the business might be vulnerable.

To think that the only time to build a business is in good times can be a mistake.

257 Believing That You Should Never Start, Expand, or Grow a Business in a Bad Economic Environment

Many managers believe that a bad economic environment is the worst time to start a business.

As counterintuitive as the idea may seem to be, an economic slump can be a very good time to start and grow a business. The reason an economic slump can actually be good for business expansion is that there is less competition for customers, key suppliers, and important talent. It is easier to be differentiated. Because hyper-growth is unlikely, a business can concentrate on fundamentals and do it right.

To think that a bad time in the economy is a bad time to start a business can be a mistake.

258 Emphasizing the Details Over Big Ideas

While details are a necessary condition to business success, details alone are not a sufficient condition to business success.

Details should not be allowed to override the importance of big ideas. If a company spends all of its time, attention, and resources on the details, the company necessarily is limited in how successful it can be. If a company is too mired in the details, so much so that it cannot address and act upon big ideas, then the company is going to be limited in what results that can be achieved.

Emphasizing details at the expense of big ideas is a mistake.

259 Insufficient Attention to Details

As much as business involves big ideas, big concepts, and big opportunities, it is also very much about details.

If companies cannot master the details, they cannot reach the highest level of success. If you don't take care of the details, then you really are not taking care of business. Business is all about the details. While details may not be a sufficient condition for success, details certainly arc a necessary condition.

To not take care of the details is a mistake.

260 Not Understanding Source of Business Outcome

Too many business people have no real understanding of how they achieve the outcomes they do.

If you do not understand how you achieve the business outcomes that you achieve, you have no ability to replicate that business outcome. If you do not understand how you get the outcome you get, you are unable to modify and adjust your approach to different circumstances and market conditions. If you do not understand how the outcome happened, your business is essentially a dice roll, rather than a purposeful, planned, managed undertaking.

If you do not understand how the outcomes you achieved were actually achieved you may be making a mistake.

261 No Performance Attribution

Performance attribution involves understanding the reasons—the why—behind particular performance.

Performance attribution involves considering the causal factors that are the reason for a particular outcome. Applied to investment management, performance attribution considers how much of the resulting investment performance is explained by the market's up or down direction, selection of industry, or selection of a specific company. By using performance attribution, it is possible to evaluate the degree to which the performance was a result of conscious, specific strategies and decisions—or mere chance. Through applying performance attribution, superior decisions and business outcomes can be achieved.

To fail to consider the implications of performance attribution is a real mistake.

262 Overnight Success

It is prevalent in popular culture to talk of overnight success.

The assumption is that because no one was aware of an individual's talent, brilliance or accomplishments before his success, then that person has become successful overnight. Not readily recognized is that the break-through musical artist labored for 20 years, practicing and practicing, traveling from club to club, working to develop and refine the sound. Although success may be recognized overnight, it seldom is the result of anything but sustained, hard work.

To think that success happens just overnight can be a mistake.

263 Dr. Phil Effect

If you ask psychologists about the success of Dr. Phil, many will insist they are better trained, more effective as therapists and more deserving of recognition than Dr. Phil McGraw, who has gained fame by being a regular on the Oprah Winfrey show, is an author of best-selling books and stars in his own TV show.

Notwithstanding how capable, hard working, deserving and motivated other psychologists might be, Dr. Phil is the one who is on Oprah, has his own show, and has the book deals. To spend time and energy bemoaning Dr. Phil's good fortune and your own lack of good fortune does nothing more than reinforce his superior market receptivity and your lack of market receptivity. Dr. Phil enjoys his favored status because of what he did to create opportunity and then to make the most of the opportunity he created.

Lamenting over the *Dr. Phil effect* is a mistake.

264 No Sense That Fame Can Be Fleeting

While fame for some is long lasting, for most it is fleeting.

If fortuitous circumstances bring fame, it is well to (1) recognize that that fame may not be permanent, (2) exploit the fame in the present, rather than presuming it will last, and (3) not make plans or commitments in reliance upon that fleeting fame being permanent. If you do not appreciate that fame is fleeting, you may miscalculate, perhaps by taking on a bigger than appropriate commitment. Alternatively, opportunities to benefit over the short-term from the fame, fleeting though it may be, may be missed. Either way, you miscalculate if you think fame is permanent. This is not to say that fame may not be permanent, but you must recognize that permanent fame is generally established by hard work and maintained by hard work. But by no means is hard work a guarantee that fame will be permanent rather than fleeting.

To count on fame being permanent rather than fleeting can be a mistake.

265 Confusing Consequences of a Positive Business Environment with Business Acumen

Some companies lack the ability to discern the difference between a good business environment and business acumen.

A good business environment has the effect of a rising tide lifting all boats. Business acumen has the capacity to do well, independent or even in spite of a challenging environment. Some executives whose companies prosper in an accommodating business environment perceive that they are skilled—metaphorically believing that they are strong bicycle riders when what they are really doing is riding downhill with a tail wind at their back.

To confuse prosperity achieved in a good business environment with business acumen can be a mistake.

266 Confusing a "Star's" Contributions with Franchise Value

Some companies confuse the value of the company franchise and the contributions that a single outstanding performer might make to the enterprise's performance.

Although in some instances an outstanding business outcome may be largely attributable to the work of a single person, most often outstanding outcome is realized not because of a single person's initiative and efforts, but as a result of the contributions of colleagues—both currently and especially those who came before—to create franchise value in the form of business platform, market position, customer relationships, brand identity and corporate resources.

Exhibit A in the case against failing to distinguish between the value of the business franchise and so-called star's contributions is the extraordinary levels of compensation paid to certain Internet analysts by Wall Street investment firms. For several years' work, a select number of analysts were paid high eight-figure compensation in the form of salary, bonuses, severance pay and other considerations for their "brilliance and contributions" to the business performance of the Wall Street firms employing them. The apparent reasoning behind such lavish compensation was that these analysts made multiples of the magnitude of their compensation in profits for their employers. But did they really? An alternative interpretation is that they happened to show up at the right place at the right time, and were fortunate to get hired to cover an exploding industry. Sometimes naivete and duplicity commanded much higher premiums than sound fiscal judgement and economic integrity.

The companies that made substantial fees providing investment banking and related financial services to the Internet companies did so because of their established franchise—their reputations, deal structuring knowledge, distribution networks, and customer relationships. If you had replaced one of the "star" analysts with another analyst, most likely the company's performance would have been only marginally impaired, and it might have even been improved. Had you replaced the company's' resources with those of a lesser-performing company, the ability of the "star" Internet analyst to create any meaningful value would be problematic, or, more likely, non-existent. What really created the value? "Star" investment analysts? or the Wall Street investment firms?

As a postscript to this sorry situation, most of the "star" investment analysts who made the high eight-figure compensation are no longer working for their firms or even in the financial services realm. And, as a consequence of their conduct, numerous Wall Street investment firms have had to pay out even greater amounts of money to settle legal claims brought against them by investors who perceived they were defrauded as a consequence of the "star" analyst's dubious, even fraudulent securities analysis.

Confusing a "star's" contributions with franchise value is a mistake.

267 Believing Truth in Labeling Applies to Business Models

Although truth in labeling laws govern advertising, those same laws do not necessarily apply to business models.

Merely because a business describes itself as being something, does not mean it is. As a case in point, Enron called itself a utility, which at one time it was, but in time it was as far from being a utility, in multiple senses of the word, as could be. You can get burned if you believe that truth in labeling applies to business models.

To think that truth in labeling applies to business models is a mistake.

268 The Reputation of the Company Is Not Necessarily Matched by the Capabilities of the People with Whom You Might Interact

Selection of a supplier, outsource provider, or key business advisor is often based on reputation.

Reputation looms large in business decisions. The common understanding is that if a company has a strong reputation, it enjoys that strong reputation because of the positive outcomes that it achieved in business over time. Yet sometimes a company with a strong reputation may have people working for it—perhaps newly hired or recently transferred from one part of the company to another—whose competence and integrity are not the same as the company's reputation. Consequently, when selecting a supplier, outsource provider, or key business advisor, it is important to consider the reputation and capabilities not just of the company itself but of the people within the company with whom you will be interacting. If you don't check out the people, you may find that the people with whom you will be working have different capabilities than the company's reputation would imply.

Failing to check out the capabilities of the people with whom you interact can be a mistake.

269 Confusing Individual Capability with Corporate Capability

Individual capability and corporate capability are not the same thing.

Merely because an individual is capable of doing something does not necessarily mean that the corporation for whom that individual works is capable of doing it. As you interact with companies in their roles as suppliers, customers, advisors, and competitors, you will do well to remember that individual capability is not company capability.

To think that individual capability is the same as company capability can be a major mistake.

270 Confusing Corporate Capability with Individual Capability

Corporations possess the capability to do things that many individuals employed by that very corporation do not have the ability to do.

The corporate capability of some corporations is sometimes traceable to a select number of individuals within that corporation who possess that capability. In other circumstances, corporate capability is attributable to and is explained by the interaction of systems, procedures, resources, training and other factors, which collectively enable people within that organization to accomplish what they otherwise could not independently do. Corporate capability is not the same as the capability of the individuals that work in the corporation. The fact that a corporation is distinguished for its capability in a particular task does not necessarily mean that individuals working for that corporation have capabilities in that particular task.

To think that corporate capability is possessed by the individuals within that corporation can be an expensive mistake.

271 Forgetting Everything Is For Sale

Too many people forget that everything is for sale. Even if you do not offer something for sale, it is for sale.

Everything is for sale, because someone could come along and offer to buy it from you. Of course, you have no obligation to accept their offer. But if you don't consider that everything is for sale, you may not have considered at what price you would sell something for. By thinking through the implications of everything being for sale, you can make better decisions, both in response to what offers may come your way and also considering whether you perhaps should sell something that you might not have otherwise thought of selling.

To forget that everything is for sale can be a mistake.

272 Considering Time a Free Good

Some companies do not recognize that time is the most precious of resources.

If time is considered a free good, companies may make decisions that impose higher costs than they recognize. Perhaps the company insists on employees filling out very time consuming reports, whose true costs, when the time to fill out the reports is considered, is much greater than the resulting value. As a consequence of such practices, employee productivity may suffer. Employees may become annoyed, disenchanted and even alienated from the company. The same thing applies to customers. If a company does not value their customers' time, then success is a long odds proposition.

To consider time a free good is a mistake.

273 Confusing Effectiveness and Efficiency

Effectiveness is concerned with *what* you do, and efficiency is concerned with *how* you do it.

Some say that effectiveness is doing the right thing while efficiency is doing it the right way. No matter how efficient you may be, if you're not effective, your outcomes will be less than distinguished. Alternatively, you can do the right thing less than efficiently and still achieve a better outcome than you would by efficiently doing wrong thing.

Confusing effectiveness with efficiency is a mistake.

274 Thinking Effectiveness Is All That Matters

Because effectiveness is more important than efficiency, some believe that effectiveness is all that matters.

As important as effectiveness is, effectiveness alone is not enough. If you are doing the right thing, but you don't do it efficiently, you are susceptible to being outperformed by a competitor who both does the right thing and does it efficiently. Efficiency—doing something with low resource costs—is very different than effectiveness—getting the right outcome.

Emphasizing effectiveness but ignoring efficiency is a mistake.

275 Playing the Timing Wrong

Things that may appear fully appropriate at one time can be entirely inappropriate another time.

Because people tend to evaluate news in the context of the times in which they encounter the news, it is important to carefully consider what you have to say in the context of the times in which you say it. Things that might at one time be perfectly appropriate and not even cause a raised eyebrow, can at another time be entirely inappropriate, so much so as to appear to reflect massive misjudgment.

Consider the situation of the CEO of the New York Stock Exchange, who, under a long-term employment contract, was paid about $100 million in 2003. Although the compensation award related to over ten years of work—in many of these years investors had prospered mightily, but in the last two or three years most had suffered large losses—when the award was announced, most had forgotten about the good times and were much more aware of and concerned about the bad times. Even though the magnitude of compensation may not have been inappropriate, given the growth and performance of the New York Stock Exchange, readers of the news story compared the $100 million figure not to compensation of other high profile CEOs and investment bankers but to the losses they had sustained on their own investment portfolios. The Chairman of the Securities and Exchange Commission demanded an explanation.

Because of poor timing, the public image of the New York Stock Exchange suffered. Instead of what might have been a positive experience of deserved recognition for a job well done, the CEO was chagrined at being the target of a less than sympathetic media. Many were amazed that the CEO of an institution that was supposedly intended to serve investors' interests could be paid so much money—especially after investors had lost so much money.

Disregarding the timing consequences of major events can be a mistake.

276 Disregarding Lessons Learned

Although many companies talk about wanting to be a learning organization, their approach to business may reflect more learning rhetoric than learning reality.

A learning organization should have a formal means of capturing what is actually learned. One approach is to encourage each individual to keep a *lessons learned* journal, recording what they have learned in the course of their work. Then, from time to time, those lessons learned can be brought together, analyzed, synthesized and distributed, so that all can benefit. If you disregard lessons learned, you may not learn very much.

To disregard lessons learned is a mistake.

277 Not Recognizing That the Show Starts Before the Curtain Goes Up

People's experience of a performance is not confined to what happens after the curtain goes up and after it goes down.

In truth, the experience of a performance encompasses what happens before the curtain goes up as well as what happens after the curtain goes down. The experience people have in learning about the show, deciding to attend, ordering the tickets, traveling to the theater, arranging for parking or transitioning from their transit, entering the theater, walking through the lobby, finding the seat, observing the theater before the performance begins, waiting for the curtain to go up—all of these pre-performance experiences influence the experience of the show itself.

Just as in a dramatic production, so, too, in business what happens before the curtain goes up is part of the experience of the show. The companies who get it right pay extraordinary attention to what happens before the curtain goes up, doing everything they can to make the experiences before the curtain goes up—and after the curtain goes down—as positive, supportive, and conducive to the audience's being in the best possible frame of mind and mood to enjoy and appreciate the show itself.

If you ignore what happens before the curtain goes up, you may be making a big mistake.

278 Failing To Be Hip

If you're in business, you had better know what's going on.

Although it used to be that to be hip was to be part of a small, rather esoteric segment of society, now being hip is the essence of business. You ignore key social and cultural trends at your peril. If you do not keep in touch with what is going on in society, then how can you offer goods and services that people will want to buy?

It is a strategic mistake to ignore the importance of being hip.

279 Forgetting That the Media Traffics in Sound Bites

What a company wants to say through an announcement is by no means what the media will choose to report.

Company executives may want to tell the whole story behind a particular development, project the implications, state all of the conditions, present the nuances, describe all of the details. After all, the development is of such significance and complexity that it is appropriate to take the time and care to tell the story fully and completely. As much as the company may wish to communicate the full, fair and complete version of the story, the reality is that the media will likely translate the story into a sound bite, which sound bite may or may not be what the company would have wanted to say. Recognizing that the media is seldom likely to take the time or care that the company would insist that its story deserves, it is preferable to communicate in the sound bites the media works with.

If you fail to consider that the media will take your story and present its sound bite version, you may make a mistake.

280 Violating Fiduciary Duty

Many companies are benignly innocent of fiduciary duty. In fact, fiduciary duty applies in more settings than many executives realize.

Fiduciary duty requires the fiduciary to put the interests of the party on whose behalf the fiduciary is acting ahead of his or her own. The fiduciary is required to make decisions that advance the other party's interests. The fiduciary is not supposed to advance his or her own interests at the expense of the party to whom the fiduciary duty is owed. Unfortunately, all too many companies do not understand this. Lacking understanding of fiduciary duty, companies may violate their fiduciary duty to others. The consequences of violating fiduciary duty can be very expensive.

To violate fiduciary duty is a mistake.

281 Prioritizing Product Over Customer

Many companies primarily focus on the product that they make or the service that they provide. Only after the company has developed the product or service does it turn its attention to how to sell the product or service.

The most successful companies have total focus and concentration on the customer. Michael Dell, CEO of the phenomenally successful firm Dell Computer, has observed that he would much rather be known for having created products that serve his customers' needs than for having created sophisticated state-of-the-art computer technology. Companies that start with the customer, considering what the customer needs and how best to meet those needs, gain greater market share, achieve more success and profitability, and create greater stock market value than do companies that emphasize the product—and consider the customer only as an afterthought.

Prioritizing product attributes over customer needs is a mistake.

282 Perceiving Fiduciary Duty as a Constraint

With the proliferation of outsourcing arrangements, whereby a company contracts with another to provide management services for an important aspect of its business, fiduciary issues and the relationships between different enterprises are of ever greater importance.

Some executives and companies, perhaps not familiar with the full ramifications of fiduciary duty, may perceive that the fiduciary duty itself is a "constraint" to pursuing profiteering activity. This perception can lead to attitudes and conduct incompatible with fiduciary duty, which could bring substantial liability to the company. A company whose executives perceive that honoring fiduciary duty is a constraint to pursuing their profiteering inclinations, could end up on the wrong side of a substantial lawsuit.

Perceiving fiduciary duty as a constraint is a mistake.

283 Negotiating a Deal Whose Payoff Is Too Deferred in Time

In a joint venture there is always a question of the timing and amount of payout. One approach is to back-end the payout, tying it to incentives, with the idea that strong performance will achieve a much higher outcome. But putting too much dependence on a future, delayed payout, tied to a very high level of outcome, can be a mistake.

Consider two different deals, negotiated on behalf of two outstanding football players, both of whom had very similar performance on the field. In one deal, a front end payment of about $8 million was negotiated, with minimal annual compensation, and very big bonus payments for achieving outstanding outcomes. Although the player had very good results, his performance fell just short of the outcomes needed to qualify for the bonus payments, so he ended up over three years making about $10 million. The other player chose a more conventional contract, but with nowhere near the upside potential that could possibly be realized by the first player. He, too, had solid results on the field. Over three years he made about $25 million. Two players, same performance, vastly different outcomes.

To negotiate a deal whose payoff is too deferred in time can be a mistake.

284 Disproportionate Emphasis on Marketing

Some companies place disproportionate emphasis on marketing, at the expense of other aspects of the business.

Marketing overemphasis reflects the thinking that marketing can overcome every other weakness. Certainly, if you have a large top line, you have the means to solve all kinds of other problems. But if you have not directed sufficient attention to other aspects of the business, ultimately, the company will implode for lack of necessary internal substance in other critical parts of the business.

An overemphasis on marketing—thinking that marketing can overcome other weaknesses—is a mistake.

285 Performance Dependent upon Decisions Made by the Other Party

In joint venture arrangements, the payout is often dependent upon future outcomes.

It is fine to have payment tied to a future outcome, so long as you largely control the circumstances that influence your ability to achieve that future outcome. But if your ability to achieve the future outcome is dependent upon decisions and actions by the other side, then your risk is much greater. If the other side chooses not to or is unable do what it is expected to do, you cannot do what you are expected to do—and you cannot achieve your expected payment.

To structure a deal that is too dependent upon the other side's performance can be a mistake.

286 Disregarding Long-term Consequences of the Deal

When structuring a deal, it is important to consider not just the short-term consequences, but the consequences of the deal over the full time span during which the deal terms might be applicable.

Companies too often make deals that appear to be reasonable in the short-term, while not considering the long-term consequences of the deal. What can be a relatively modest payment over a short time span can grow to a massive payment over the long term. Because of changing circumstances over time, reasonable terms can become totally unreasonable.

Consider the arrangement whereby part of a chief executive officer's compensation was a payment of 2% of revenues. With $10 million dollars of revenues, this particular contractual provision amounts to $200,000. But if revenues were to grow to $2 billion, perhaps through a series of mergers and acquisitions, this contract provision would amount to $40 million. While in some instances it may be totally appropriate to pay the CEO $40 million per year, this level of compensation may be neither justified nor appropriate in every circumstance.

If you do not consider the long-term consequences you may make a mistake.

287 Too Busy to Read

Some executives assert that they are working so hard that they are simply too busy to read.

Executives who say that they are too busy to read run the risk of missing out on a lot that they might not otherwise encounter: new ideas, new thinking and new strategies. Possibly, these new ideas, new thinking and new strategies could lead to insights that could have a dramatic impact upon their company's performance. Reading can lead to new ways of looking at things, to connecting with past truths that may have been forgotten or neglected, to seeing new ways to frame existing circumstances, and to insights that can lead to opportunities in the future. Reading can enhance perspective, promote inspiration and deepen understanding.

Executives who fail to read make a mistake.

MARKETING AND SALES

288 Marketing Myopia

Legendary Harvard Business School marketing Professor Ted Levitt labeled the lack of focus on the marketplace as "marketing myopia."

In a classic *Harvard Business Review* article, Levitt told the story of how railroads perceived that they were in the railroad business rather than the transportation business. Consequently, first the trucking companies emerged to take major market share and then airlines emerged to take major market share. This myopic perspective of the market is reflected in concentration on the operations of the business rather than on customer benefit and experience. Marketing myopia leads to loss of leadership in the market.

Myopia about your markets is a mistake.

289 Thinking You're Not in the Marketing Business

All too many companies think they are in every business but the marketing business.

In truth, every company is in the marketing business. And then, after the marketing business, the company is in the business of making something, selling something, and/or providing some service. Sure, the company is about its basic business of making, selling, or servicing, but if the company does not engage in marketing—to attract and retain customers—the company will have no real opportunity to make, sell or provide services. Marketing is a precondition to doing whatever the company basically does. So every company is first in the marketing business.

To think you are not in the marketing business is a mistake.

290 Marketing Underemphasis

Companies that underemphasize marketing do so to their peril.

A company may be so involved in its production process, dealing with internal organization issues, coping with technology considerations, and the like, that it devotes too few resources to marketing. Too few resources devoted to marketing means that the company will fall far short of the performance that it might realize, were sufficient resources devoted to marketing.

Underemphasizing marketing is a mistake.

291 Too Much Self-Confidence

Strong leaders necessarily operate with a high level of self-confidence. After all, if you don't believe in yourself, why should anyone else?

As important as self-confidence is, it can be a mistake to be too self-confident. If you underestimate your opponent, you may be in for a surprise. Too much self-confidence, leading to a *take-it-for-granted-no-need-to-prepare* approach, can be precarious. If you do not do sufficient preparation, you may find your self-confidence is unwarranted. You may be surprised, perhaps expensively, even disastrously.

Too much self-confidence can be a major mistake.

292 Thinking Pricing Solves All Problems

For some companies, pricing is their dominant emphasis.

Price focused companics bclicvc that if they can just undercut the competition by a little bit, that will be enough to attract customers and generate sales. Such companies mistakenly ignore the reality that there is always going to be someone who will—at least temporarily if not permanently — accept a lower margin and provide lower quality. Alternatively, the company may think that by just moving their prices up enough, they can achieve the revenues and margins they wish. But, price is not all there is. Price must be related to the quality of what is offered, the company's brand, its internal economics and competitive considerations.

Thinking that pricing is a panacea to all problems is a mistake.

293 Obsessing About Market Share

Some companies become obsessed with market share.

The obsession with market share follows from the thinking that companies that are market leaders tend to achieve higher levels of financial performance than do those that are market laggards. Some take this to mean that by maximizing market share, you are, by definition, the market leader. Not so fast. Market share dominance can be synonymous with market leadership, but not necessarily. It is important to consider whether the leading market share is matched by leading customer relationships, high product and service quality, sustainable competitive advantage and superior financial performance.

To be obsessed with market share can be a mistake.

294 Disconnect Between Engineering and Sales

A classic challenge in business is to connect engineering and sales. When engineering and sales are connected and coordinated, businesses can thrive. When they are not, businesses can and do flounder.

A challenge in connecting engineering and sales is that the two have different priorities. Engineers can become fascinated by an engineering problem whose solution may be intellectually ingenious but of limited interest to the customer. The sales perspective is to represent what the customer really wants and is willing to pay for. The problem in connecting engineering and sales is that what can easily be produced is not necessarily what customers want—and what customers want cannot necessarily be easily produced. If sales and engineering are not balanced and coordinated, the business suffers.

A disconnect between sales and engineering can be a mistake.

295 Utilizing Inappropriate Marketing Research

Marketing research can only be as effective as the appropriateness of the methodologies employed.

If you employ a methodology inappropriate to the issues you are researching, the likelihood of getting useful, insightful outcomes is reduced. One favored market research technique to evaluate new products and ideas is the focus group, a group of people who participate in a guided discussion to get their reactions to a particular new idea, product or service. But if the idea, product or service has significant emotional content—which may be more readily accessed at the unconscious level than the explicit conscious level—engaging in dialogue may be of relatively limited effectiveness. It may be better to employ alternative processes, such as asking people to draw visual images or to identify pictures in magazines that convey their feelings and sentiments, than to rely upon an approach that is not well suited to access the really important insights and information.

Inappropriate marketing research can be a mistake.

296 What You Didn't Sell Today You Bought at the Price That You Could Sell It For

In stock market investing, there is a saying that any stock not sold today was effectively bought at the price it could have been sold for. The same concept applies in business.

In terms of employees, customers, machinery, product, inventory, business divisions and more, the basic ideas is that every day you have the opportunity to make a decision to sell any aspect of the business. Anything you choose not to sell, you effectively bought for the price that you could have sold it for. Often companies find that if they think explicitly about what price they could sell something for, they make better decisions.

If you fail to consider that what you didn't sell today you bought at the price you could have sold it for, you may be making a mistake.

297 Ignoring Place

Although place is one of the critical five P's of marketing—along with product, pricing, packaging and promotion—it is too often ignored.

Ignoring the role of place in marketing is a perilous proposition, especially today, when people can be ever more choiceful about the places in which they choose to live, work, learn, play, shop and prosper. Place is very important for marketing in terms of how customers access the product or service. Further, place considerations are central to three-dimensional marketing, where the location and the actual physical structure of the business convey important marketing messages. And, with experiences being an increasingly valued attribute of the customer's purchase expectations and enjoyment, the contribution that place makes to the experience of the purchase and the product looms large.

Marketing that discounts the importance of place represents a mistake.

298 Cutting Advertising and Sales when the Economy Slows

When a difficult economy impacts a company's financial performance, it is natural to look to ways to cope with the financial pressure.

One way companies cope with financial pressure is to reduce costs. A favored target for cost reduction is advertising and sales staff. The argument goes that since the company's financial performance is suffering, the company can no longer afford the luxury of advertising. And if sales are going to be down, then certainly the company does not need as many people selling. Wrong. When it is more difficult to get sales, that is precisely the time that the business should devote more resources to pursuing sales. Cutting back on marketing activity in a weak economic environment can cause business performance to suffer even more.

Reducing marketing expenses in a difficult economic environment can be a mistake.

299 Too Much Business Promotion

Sometimes a company with a strong customer base is approached by other companies desiring to access that customer base to do deals.

Just as it can be a mistake to fail to exploit the opportunities resident in company's client relationships, so, too, can it be a mistake to engage in excessive business promotion to that client base. Too much promotion to a client base can diminish the value of that client base. After all, if you put too many billboards in a neighborhood, the people in that neighborhood—whose presence is the reason the billboard advertiser wanted to be there in the first place—may find the billboard-saturated neighborhood a less than appealing place to live. And selling messages that would have been effective in a less saturated neighborhood are no longer even noticed.

Too much promotion to your core customer base can be a mistake.

300 Using Conventional Media to Reach an Unconventional Audience

Companies that aspire to innovation, but employ traditional methods to get there, must recognize that they are more likely to be disappointed than pleased by their outcomes.

Consider the company that wished to reach a non-traditional audience, which audience had the common denominator of being opinion leaders, but who otherwise did not show up in any concentrated way in traditional market classifications. The company proceeded to pursue a traditional advertising promotion campaign, emphasizing heavy print and television, but the results were very disappointing. The company did not recognize that if you wish to reach a non-traditional buyer, you must use non-traditional media and non-traditional promotion and selling methods.

Seeking a different outcome, but using undifferentiated means in pursuing it, can be a mistake.

301 Primary Reliance on a Single Sales and Marketing Method

Some companies rely predominantly on a single sales and marketing method.

Having been very successful with that single sales and marketing method, the company perceives no reason to do anything differently. After all, why fix what is not broken? But if you rely upon a single sales and marketing method, no matter how successful that method may have been in the past, you may find that you are very vulnerable. Maybe conditions in the market change. Maybe new competition renders your prior successful sales and marketing method ineffective. Maybe new technology makes other methods more effective. Maybe regulations constrain or prohibit your ability to employ that one successful sales and marketing method.

To rely exclusively on a single sales and marketing method is a mistake.

302 Wishing Someone Else Would Solve Your Sales Problem

Numerous companies have significant underutilized capacity and wish for a sales solution so they could utilize that capacity.

Seeking to raise their sales performance, the company may hire a sales superstar to solve the problem. While sometimes this approach works, more often than not these optimistic expectations are disappointed. Because the lack of sales results are usually attributable to many factors, unless all significant factors influencing sales performance are addressed, sales are unlikely to improve meaningfully merely as a consequence of hiring a sales pro. Wishing someone would solve your sales problem is an abdication of responsibility. If the company does not take the initiative to solve its own sales problem, it will not be solved.

Wishing for someone to come in and take care of your own sales problem is a mistake.

303 Thinking Geography Is a Market Barrier

It used to be that geography served as a market barrier. Companies not in your geographic area did not compete with you. But no more.

Today, geography is seldom a market barrier. Information, ideas, talent, people, products, and raw materials move rapidly from one place to another. Even products that are characterized by substantial bulk and weight—such as steel and automobiles, that seemingly would be more competitively advantageous to produce close to home than far away—move easily from distant places to far away markets. Geography is no longer a barrier.

If you think geography is a market barrier, you are making a big mistake.

304 Lack of Clarity About Your Market

Too many businesses lack clarity about their market.

How can you tell if a business lacks clarity about its market? A good starting point is to look at its ads. In the majority of business advertising, it is difficult to discern who the business wants to reach with that ad. While some businesses may appeal to everyone, the vast majority do not. If you cannot tell from the company's marketing message who the company does *not* wish to appeal to, then you probably cannot tell who the company wishes to appeal to. If the company doesn't know what it wants, how can it expect its customers to know?

Failing to be clear about your market is a mistake.

305 Seeking to Be All Things to All People

Many companies are desperately frightened that they may miss out on a customer.

Not wanting to miss out on a customer, companies may cast a wide net, hoping to attract the customer they fear they might miss with a narrower approach. In doing this, the company essentially is seeking to be all things to all people. While in earlier times, with fewer choices, limited communications, and unsophisticated customers, perhaps one provider could meet many of the needs of a substantial number of customers. No more. Today, seeking to be all things to all people is more likely to end up being few or no things to a majority of people.

Seeking to be all things to all people is a mistake.

306 Failing to Differentiate Between Customers and Prospects

Companies that fail to differentiate between customers and prospects may lose the patronage of the first and never achieve the patronage of the second.

A customer is an individual or company with whom you are already doing business. A prospect is someone you have identified that you might do business with, but have yet to do so. Customers have different expectations and needs than do prospects. The approach and treatment that would be appropriate for someone you have yet to do business with is not the same approach you should use with someone you are already doing business with.

Failing to differentiate between the needs and expectations of customers and prospects is a mistake.

307 Treating Customers and Prospects Alike

Some companies have the idea that everyone they might encounter in a business setting is an equal and should be treated equally. Not so.

Customers, by virtue of their past relationship, have already proven that they have made the decision to buy from you. Customers have moved much farther along the spectrum from *awareness of what you do* to the *commitment to engage in business with you* than have prospects. Sales research has concluded that it costs six times more in resources to convert someone you have not done business with to a customer, than to sell something additional to an existing customer. It follows that the same amount of resources devoted to your existing customers would generate six times the sales as those resources devoted to prospects with whom you have yet to do business. But all too many companies allocate their resources the opposite way—spending much more on prospects than customers.

If you treat your existing customers the same way you treat your prospects, you may be making a mistake.

308 Treating All Customers Alike

Some companies treat all their customers alike.

Companies that treat all of their customers alike provide the same level of service and attention to the customer who spends a small amount with the company as they devote to the customer that spends a much larger amount with the company. Although treating all customers alike may promote concepts of equality, it is not necessarily good business. Often the customer that buys only a small amount from the company is not a very profitable business relationship, for it may cost more to service that customer than the company makes off the customer. Customers who spend a great deal with the company are the source of the company's profits. If you fail to acknowledge the customers who are the primary contributors to your profits, you may find that the customer's attention drifts away and your profits drift away, too.

Treating all customers alike is a mistake.

309 Devoting Too Many Resources to Unqualified Prospects

Some businesses devote such a level of resources to unqualified prospects that they are unable to spend sufficient attention on qualified prospects.

If a prospect is unqualified, the sooner you can help that prospect direct his or her energies to a more rewarding direction, the better for you and the better for the prospect. Wasting someone's time and resources, in responding to something that will ultimately not be of interest to him, is not only disrespectful to him but also an inefficient use of your own resources. The sooner a company can eliminate the unqualified to focus on the most qualified, the more likely that company can be successful. Some of the most effective companies consciously seek to discourage the unqualified from having anything to do with them.

Devoting too many resources to unqualified prospects is a mistake.

310 Not Knowing Your Customers

While many companies talk about how important their customers are to them, a surprising number of these companies don't really know much about these customers. Knowledge of customers is absolutely crucial to business success.

Some marketing pros argue that the most important assets any business has are its customers and customer relationships. If you do not have critical information about your customers—their attributes, demographic factors and buying patterns—your business is of only limited value. Valuable businesses have strong customer relationships, which they nurture, deepen and enrich, by continually engaging in valuable, meaningful communications with their customers.

Not knowing your customers is a mistake.

311 Failing to Appreciate That Customers Are Different From You

The attributes crucial to successful leadership of enterprises may be very different from the characteristics of the broad marketplace.

Executives who perceive that their market shares the same values as they do, may miscalculate. Many leaders are more independent than dependent, more inclined to go their own way than to be swayed by peer pressure, and more likely to desire the unconventional than to conform and belong to the crowd. But the market that the company sells to may, in fact, be precisely what that leader is not. If the leader is unable to understand and respond to the mindset of the customer—that leader may well miscalculate.

Thinking that the customer is just like you can be a mistake.

312 Failing to Recognize That Not All Customers Are the Same

Although customers share certain common attributes, in many important ways customers may be very different.

To think that because customers share certain common attributes they do not differ meaningfully from each other, can be a real miscalculation. Customers' unique circumstances, resources, motivations, pressures and concerns can lead them to buy for very different reasons and at very different times. If you do not understand the uniqueness of your customers, you may not only lose opportunities for specific business transactions, but even lose the relationship.

Failing to recognize that not all customers are the same can be a mistake.

313 Insensitivity to Customer Relationships

Customer relationships are crucial in business.

Companies that are insensitive to customer relationships—failing to appreciate how crucially important they are—may find that their ability to achieve their objectives is materially compromised. After all, in many ways, you succeed in life because of others—sometimes in spite of, sometimes independently of, sometimes directly as a consequence of. A profile in *Fortune* magazine of a successful real estate developer described the developer as being "successful because you want him to be successful." The story made the point that he achieved success because of his positive personal relationships.

Insensitivity to customer relationships is a mistake.

314 Failing to Understand the Lifetime Value of a Customer

Too few businesses understand the lifetime value of a customer.

The lifetime value of a customer is the expected value of the customer to the business over time. The lifetime value calculation involves consideration of average transaction size, frequency of transactions, expected continuity, profit margin per transaction, cost of providing continuing customer service and retention, and the net benefits from probable referrals. Many companies are surprised to discover that the lifetime value of a customer is many times the profit of a specific transaction. If you do not know the lifetime value of a customer, you may make less than astute decisions concerning customer acquisition and retention.

Although a customer may engage in one transaction at a time with a company, many customers will engage in multiple transactions over their lifetime relationship with the company. Companies that interact with customers in the context of a single transaction, rather than in terms of the economics of the lifetime relationship, may egregiously miscalculate. A company may not want to spend the resources required to create the customer relationship in the first place. The company may make a short-term penny-wise, long-term pound-foolish decision concerning a particular customer issue. A company may sacrifice substantial long-term customer value by miscalculating in a way that serves a short-term objective.

Miscomprehending the lifetime value of a customer is a significant mistake.

315 Concentrating Primarily on New Customers

Most businesses that are committed to growth concentrate on achieving that growth by adding new customers.

For many companies, the primary source of growth is new customers. But it can be a mistake to concentrate too much on new customers at the expense of existing customers. It costs much more resources to acquire a new customer than to retain an existing customer. By both adding new customers and retaining existing customers, a company can achieve substantially greater growth than if it does only one of the two.

Emphasizing adding new customers at the expense of existing customers is a mistake.

316 Thinking a Customer's Order Is a Final Sale

Just because a customer places an order, that does not mean the order will actually be realized as a sale.

To understand what is involved in delivering a customer's order, you have to work backwards, up the supply chain to the source. The problem in matching customer orders and production is that not every order turns out to be a sale. Perhaps the customer's business changes, and slower sales and/or cost-cutting directives from above cause cancellation of orders. Or alternatively, figuring that hyper-demand may result in supply shortages, some customers may consciously over-order from multiple suppliers, counting on such over-orders to increase their chances of getting the desired delivery. Once assured of the delivery, these customers cancel the unneeded orders.

In situations susceptible to hyper-demand, which might result in supply shortages, companies accepting orders need to take whatever steps necessary to confirm that it is a real order.These steps may include a legal commitment, payment in advance, or some other arrangement to protect the company from the customer placing a big order that he has no real intention to taking delivery on. The company needs to do what is necessary to deal with what the customer regards as an expression of interest to confirm it can get what it wants, and the company's substantial financial commitment to fulfill what may turn out to be a phantom order.

It can be an expensive mistake, resulting in excessive inventory buildup, to think that a customer order is in fact a sale.

317 Trading Responsiveness to Customers for Lower Manufacturing Costs

To drive costs down, many companies have moved manufacturing offshore, to distant locations.

By concentrating manufacturing in places of lower labor and associated costs, the unit production costs of goods can be reduced meaningfully. However, a significant but all too little appreciated consequence of distance manufacturing is the reduced capacity to respond to customer desires. If you can get your product into the store quickly, and thereby persuade customers to buy more frequently and at higher volume, increased turnover can possibly more than offset the incremental higher manufacturing costs. An emphasis on lower manufacturing costs can result in long lags in getting the product into the store. By the time the product gets to the store, demand may be less than vibrant. So even though the cost is lower, fewer sales result.

Emphasizing lower costs at the expense of responsiveness to customers can be a mistake.

318 Failing to Appreciate That Your Apparent Competitor May Really Be Your Customer

The distinction between customers and competitors used to be straightforward. Today, however, no longer are the identities of customers and competitors so easily distinguishable. Increasingly, a company that may be a competitor in one aspect of the business may be a customer in another aspect. If you fail to appreciate this realignment of company interrelationships, you may grievously miscalculate.

A senior executive of a hotel company once complained to a partner of an accounting firm that he was very unhappy that the accounting firm had appeared as an expert in a legal matter opposite his hotel company. The partner explained that the hotel company had never hired his accounting firm for any professional services, so therefore he felt no loyalty to that hotel company and there was no reason not to appear on behalf of clients who wanted to hire his firm. The partner further pointed out to the hotel executive that the accounting firm was the hotel company's second largest customer throughout the world, as the accounting firm used that hotel for a substantial meeting business. To his chagrin, the hotel executive realized that he had been attacking one of his very best customers, whose patronage represented a substantial portion of the hotel company's profits.

If you fail to consider that an apparent competitor in one part of your business may be a prime customer in another, you may make a major mistake.

319 Pursuing a Technology Solution That Serves a Narrow Set of the Customers

Many companies, in the quest to satisfy and respond to their customers' needs and desires, pursue enhancements and improvements of their products.

In expanding a product's capabilities and enhancing its features, the challenge is to determine whether the enhancements will satisfy a few customers or many customers. Merely because one customer asks for something does not necessarily mean that all or the majority of other customers will want that additional feature. Investing substantial resources to add a feature that appeals to only a small segment of the customer base may be an uneconomic undertaking.

Developing a product enhancement that appeals to only a small number of customers can be a mistake.

320 Placing Your Own Interest Above and In Conflict with Your Commitments to Your Customers

In many business arrangements, companies create fiduciary relationships with their customers. Under a fiduciary relationship, the company is obligated to place its customer's interests ahead of its own.

Some companies seem to be confused about the implications of fiduciary relationship. In one instance, a company claimed that its right to serve as a manufacturer's representative—which right was intended to enable it to operate more effectively on behalf of its customer—justified it being able to charge the customer whatever fees it chose to charge, irrespective of other commitments and provisions of the underlying agreement. In spite of the company's representations and justifications, the customer was motivated to take its business elsewhere.

Placing your own interests above and in conflict with your commitments to your customers is a mistake.

321 Primary Dependence upon a Single Customer

A company that depends primarily on a single customer is at great risk.

If a company depends on a single customer, the company is vulnerable to what might happen to that customer. What if the customer goes out of business? What if new management or personnel changes with that customer causes them to be disinclined to do business with you? What if the customer demands extraordinary price concessions that destroy your ability to make a fair profit and return on your investment? If you have too much dependence on a single customer, you may find yourself out of business.

To rely primarily on a single customer is a major mistake.

322 Lacking Customer Contact Information

While many companies talk about how important their customers are to them, very few companies have the necessary contact information that they need to actually contact their customers.

Unless a customer is somehow reading the company promotion materials and the articles in which managers proclaim how important the customers are to the company, how would customers ever know? To have strong customer relationships, you must have customer contact information. If you do not have customer contact information, you cannot initiate customer contact. Complete, accurate, timely customer contact information is a precondition to being in a position to implement effective customer-centered marketing communications.

If you lack customer contact information, you are making a mistake.

323 Not Contacting Your Customers

The saying, "out of sight, out of mind," can be adapted to the business equivalent of "out of contact, out of mind."

If you are not contacting your customers, you are not likely at the top of their mind. If your customers are not hearing from you, then your customers are probably not thinking of you. If a company does not contact its customers, the priority of that company to that customer is inevitably diminished. Eventually, over time, a company that was once very important to a customer may fade away from that customer's consciousness.

Losing customers as a consequence of not contacting them is a mistake.

324 Confusion Regarding Target Customer

Many businesses seem to be confused about their target customers.

The company may say it wants to do business with anybody that is interested in what it has to offer. Does that mean every name in the phone book is a legitimate priority target for this company? If the company is not clear concerning its customer targets, the company is not in the position to design offers to appeal to those customers. If the company is not clear about its customer targets, the company is not in the position to communicate effectively to those customers. If the company is not clear about its customer targets, the company cannot be nearly as successful as it could be.

Confusion concerning customer targets is a mistake.

325 Not Understanding Why Customers Buy from You

Customers buy from companies for any number of reasons. Often, the reason the company thinks a customer buys is very different than why the customers really buy.

If you do not understand the real reasons that customers buy from you, you may make decisions that are based upon your reasons, not the customers' reasons. If you do not consider the customers' point of view when you make decisions, you may make decisions that are contrary to the customers' desires, interests and objectives. If you do that too often, you may lose your customers.

Not understanding why customers buy from you is a mistake.

326 Selling Them What You Want Them to Want—Rather Than What They Want

Many companies are so in love with their product that they pay scant attention to what their customers really want.

Some businesses are entirely product-driven and concentrate solely on the product, believing that if they produce a good product then customers will naturally want that product. Others take a different approach, seeking to understand what their customers want and then determining whether there can be a good fit between the company's product offerings and the customers' desires. By considering customers' needs and wants, these companies can produce a product that is more responsive to customer desires. Not surprisingly, companies who pay attention to what customers want tend to be much more successful than those who do not.

Selling only what you want your customers to want—rather than what they want—is a mistake.

327 Unbalanced Product Offer

A company must maintain a balance between the value delivered to the customer and the value delivered to the shareholder.

If you deliver too much value to the customer, so that the company cannot make money, the company will no longer be able to serve that customer. But if you deliver too little value to the customer, so that the customer is not satisfied and does not return, the company will likewise suffer. This is why the meat cutter is the most important person working in a steakhouse. If the serving is too large, the steakhouse loses money. If the serving is too small, the steakhouse loses customers. Getting it right—satisfying both the customers and the profit objective—is crucial.

If you are unbalanced in meeting customer and company needs, you are making a mistake.

328 Too Much Emphasis on Selling Price

When you are selling something, when you get paid can be as important as how much you get paid.

Some sellers concentrate predominantly on selling price, rather than the timing of payment. If you are selling something, a lower price paid in cash right away or perhaps even in advance may be better than a higher price paid later. A savvy seller is concerned not just with the selling price, but payment timing and terms.

Concentrating on selling price without sufficiently considering payment timing is a mistake.

329 Compromising Quality in Search of Lower Price

In many industries aggressive price competition is a primary means of attracting customers.

Price pressure is usually especially intense in businesses that are highly competitive, with many companies seeking the same customer. In difficult economic conditions, price competition can be even more severe. But compromising quality to offer a lower price can be a real miscalculation, particularly as it can lead to the inability to retain customers, possible negative word-of-mouth that can compromise attracting new customers, and even liability—if the product fails to perform to represented standards.

Compromising quality in the quest to provide the lowest possible price can be a mistake.

330 Inconsistent Product and Service Quality

Consistency in product and service quality is critically important.

If a company is inconsistent in product quality and customer service, it is very difficult to attract and retain customers. A customer that first encounters a company on a bad-quality day will be unlikely to return. And that customer may be the messenger of adverse word-of-mouth about the company. If the customer happens to encounter the company on a good-quality day, that customer is susceptible to defection once they encounter a bad-quality day. Successful customer relations and companies are built by consistent product quality and customer experience.

Inconsistent customer service and product quality are mistakes.

331 Coping with Weak Market Conditions by Cutting Product Quality

When market conditions are weak, one response some companies turn to is to cut back on expenses.

One area of expenses some companies seek to cut back is product quality, with the motivation that every dollar saved is a dollar added to the bottom line. The rationalization behind cutting back product quality is that the current level of quality may be unnecessary or the customer may not really miss it.

In one instance, a large international construction company—when faced with a challenging economic environment and less demand for its proposed building development projects—chose to reduce the quantity of steel used in girders to support a large building. What the company did not consider sufficiently is that the reduced quantity of steel support for the building weakened the building's fundamental engineering integrity. When a major earthquake occurred, the building collapsed, resulting in major economic losses, loss of reputation, and subsequent expensive litigation.

Coping with weak market conditions by cutting back on product quality can be a mistake.

332 Ignoring the Importance of the Top Line

The top line of the business is critically important.

If the company does not place predominant priority on the top line—on generating revenue—it will inevitably underperform. Astute chief executive officers know that their primary priority is the top line. If the top line is taken care of, then everything else is possible. If the top line is not there, no matter how good the company is in other parts of the business, disappointment, if not failure, is inevitable.

Disregarding the importance of the top line is a mistake.

333 Marketing Mush

Some companies pay a lot of attention to marketing, but what they end up doing is engaging in marketing mush, as opposed to marketing effectiveness.

Marketing mush is throwing a lot of stuff in and calling it marketing. Marketing mush results from embracing one marketing idea and another marketing idea and whatever marketing innovation or new concept that may come along. All those many marketing ideas are thrown together. There is no clarity, no coordination, no integration in the company's marketing. Although the individual elements may alone be worthwhile, even meritorious, collectively they form a mush, without much flavor, texture or taste.

Marketing mush is a mistake.

334 Too Slow to Introduce New Products

If a company is too slow to introduce new products, it may find that it loses customer relationships, market share, and value.

Although some business sectors may be so established and uncompetitive that innovation is of no concern, the majority of business sectors are characterized by continual product innovation. Indeed, in some leading companies, as much as half of the product line may be turned over within five years. If a company is slow to introduce new products, it may find that its business stature deteriorates, perhaps slowly at first, but then more rapidly.

Companies that are too slow to introduce new products may be making a mistake.

335 Jumping on the Innovation Bandwagon

Today, it seems that innovation is the mantra of every organization.

The business press and management journals urge individuals to be creative and companies to be innovative. Certainly, innovation and creativity are important. But to think that every person is likely to provide significant innovative and creative contributions to the organization—or that every organization is going to make meaningful creative and innovative contributions—is a major miscalculation. Innovation and creativity are specialized, rather than common, talents.

To think that 'any' organization, including yours, can be just as creative and innovative as any other organization, can be a mistake.

336 Thinking Innovation Is Happenstance

Some believe that innovation is happenstance, not readily susceptible to a managerial approach.

Although some innovation appears to be happenstance, and some innovation certainly is totally unexpected, innovation can, in fact, be managed. By "managed," this is not to suggest that one can order up innovation just as one orders up a part from the supply room. But you can apply a managerial approach to innovative processes and innovation programs. A managerial approach to innovation involves not leaving innovation to chance but deliberating, studying what conditions are most conducive to innovation, and then taking the necessary steps to put in place the circumstances that may make innovation most likely. By taking a managerial approach to innovation, you can increase the likelihood of it happening and the pervasiveness of its impact.

Thinking that innovation is only a happenstance outcome is a mistake.

337 Thinking Innovation Doesn't Take Hard Work

Although the popular view of innovation is that it just somehow happens spontaneously, in truth, innovation takes hard work.

Innovation involves conscientious, deliberate, painstaking, detailed work. As a general proposition, the more information, the more exposure to ideas, the more training and preparation that a person has, the more innovative that person can be. If you forsake all of the hard work involved in innovation, believing that it just happens spontaneously, you are likely miscalculating.

Thinking that innovation does not involve hard work is a mistake.

338 Emphasizing Social Capital at the Expense of Innovation

Social capital and innovation can be in conflict.

Social capital embraces all the social arrangements and networks that enable people to work together collaboratively and cooperatively. Social capital is the essence of community. But the more social capital is emphasized, the more difficult innovation may be. Innovation, by contrast, often can be contrary to social capital, inasmuch as it challenges recognized norms and established ways of doing things. Too much priority on social capital can frustrate and inhibit innovation.

To place too much emphasis on social capital over innovation can be a mistake.

339 Failure of Imagination

Failures research has confirmed that more companies fail because of a lack of imagination than because of excessive, unjustified optimism.

Failure of imagination is reflected in small thinking, in the inability to see a better, larger tomorrow, and in the incapability of imagining a much different and grander future. Failure of imagination means that what might have been, if only the company had thought about it and prepared for it, never will be.

Failure of imagination is a big mistake.

ORGANIZATION

340 Too Many Layers of Management

Essential to the function of management is breaking down tasks and activities into smaller components, which are then assigned to business units to perform. Then the work assigned to the smaller units needs to be consolidated, brought together and taken to the senior executive and board level of the organization, for decision and action.

If a company employs too many layers of management, there are too many layers through which information and decisions must pass before consideration and action can be taken. The timeliness and quality of decisions may suffer. Too many layers of management can breed bureaucracy and unresponsiveness.

Too many layers of management is a mistake.

341 Too Many Reports

In classic management literature, seven reporting relationships was viewed as the largest number that a manager could effectively supervise in the course of day-to-day work.

Changes in organizational thinking have resulted in many managers supervising not just more than seven individuals, but multiples of seven. Now, 15, 20 or even 30 or more direct reports from individuals is not unusual. Certainly, the manager's effectiveness in dealing with multiple reports is influenced by many factors, including the nature of the work, the personalities and locations of the individuals involved, the management system, and the quality of information available to support the management system. How many direct reports a manager has necessarily influences how much time the manager might spend with each of those individuals. Too many reports can strain a manager's ability to deal with individuals and constrain the organization's effectiveness.

Too many reports can be a mistake.

342 A Too-Flat Organization

Management thinking in recent years has advocated weeding out management layers of the organization, to make it more flat.

A flat organization, with fewer levels of management, results in the managers and executives having a larger number of reports. In a flat organization, managers must address issues that in a layered organization were addressed by others. In many instances, a flat organization can achieve more responsive decision making. But sometimes, a flatter organization can backfire, causing performance to suffer, as the managers are overwhelmed by too much to comprehend and act upon, with the results that customers, employees, and key relationships receive less attention than they desire and deserve.

Too flat an organization can be a mistake.

343 Using Linear Language to Communicate Emotional Concepts

The language employed for communications can often determine the outcome of those communications.

If the subject of the communication involves feelings and emotional issues, it can be a mistake to employ linear language to communicate those issues. By employing linear language to communicate issues that are inherently non-linear, you risk a disconnect in the communication process, as the communications may be compromised and confused, rather than clear and coherent. Communications in which the intent, tone, sentence structure and vocabulary matches the subject matter is superior to communications in which there is a disconnect between the style and the subject matter.

Using linear language in communicating about non-linear issues can be a mistake.

344 Failing to Talk Straight

These days it seems that blunt, straight talk occurs all too seldom.

With the emphasis on political and cultural correctness, emotional sensitivity, and not being too overbearing or heavy handed, language can be watered down. Rather than being straightforward and direct, the vocabulary can be roundabout, convoluted, non-linear, or even crooked. When straight talk is called for, the language should be straight, plain, direct, and unambiguous.

Failing to talk straight when straight talk is called for is a mistake.

345 Too Many Group Meetings

Although much of management takes place in group settings, too much time spent in meetings can preclude getting much of anything done.

As important as it is to get people together to coordinate their efforts, too much time spent on coordination can mean that nobody ever gets much of anything done, as people become bored, distracted, disinterested or stuck in a rut. Research has shown that creative work is much more likely to happen when one person works alone or interacts with a small number of people, rather than in large groups.

Spending too much time in meetings can be a mistake.

346 Too Little Coordination

As important as it is to be decisive and quick-moving in business, if insufficient attention is directed to coordination, the results can suffer.

In conditions characterized by complexity, change and uncertainty, coordination is especially important. Coordination is necessary to assure that people do not work at cross-purposes, pursue avenues that are inherently unrewarding, and generally conduct themselves in ways that reflect a lack of coordination.

Insufficient attention to coordination can be a mistake.

347 Too-Homogeneous Management Team

While it is important that the management team has basic compatibility, if the management team is too homogeneous the company may be less than effective.

A too homogeneous management team can result in everybody thinking, saying, and doing the same thing. New ideas, new approaches and new ways of doing things are rejected, or often not even considered. If the management team is too homogeneous, there may be no receptivity to new thinking, which new thinking could improve the company's overall performance.

Too homogeneous a management team can be a mistake.

348 Mismatch of Managerial Styles

Different companies have different managerial styles.

If a company's mix of managerial styles clashes, the effectiveness of the management team may be affected. If divergent managerial styles cause executives to be at cross purposes—pulling in opposite directions rather than together—the company's ability to accomplish its objectives is inevitably less than if the managerial styles of the executives are more compatible.

Operating a business with a mismatch of managerial styles can be a mistake.

349 No Successor Management Plan

Astute companies operate with a successor management plan.

A successor management plan identifies, for each of the critical positions in the company, the logical person to be selected in the event something might happen to the person currently in that position. By anticipating in advance the replacement person, the successor management plan avoids the stress and complications of designating a replacement after someone is no longer there. In a way, the successor management plan combines both a *forward-looking* approach to management and an *expect the best, plan for the worst* orientation.

Not to have a successor management plan is a mistake.

350 CEO Doesn't Really Care

If people perceive that the CEO doesn't really care about the business, they are going to be less likely to want to be part of the business.

In one company the CEO adopted a very distant, hands-off style. He spent more of his time trout fishing than tending to the affairs of the business. Because he was essentially remote and inaccessible, decisions that might have happened within a few days or a week or two would drag on for many, many months. Morale and productivity suffered.

It is a mistake for a company to have a CEO who doesn't care.

351 CEO Lacks Passion

If the CEO is not vitally, intensely and passionately involved in the business, the company is unlikely to be as successful as it could.

Passion is important, as it communicates to employees, customers, and important members of the business community that the company really cares. If the CEO is not passionate, why should anybody else be passionate? Passion conveys enthusiasm, excitement, and commitment. A passionate CEO can take a company places that the less intensely involved CEO will never get to.

It is a mistake to have a company led by a CEO who lacks passion.

352 Emphasizing Unidimensional Performance Measurement

Performance measurement has historically involved one dimension.

A managerial approach that emphasizes one dimension, as contrasted to multiple dimensions, is inherently limiting. More and more, organizations and their leaders are expected to deliver performance that is not readily reflected in a single measurement approach. Rather, multiple measurement criteria are needed. Measuring sales performance solely by the absolute dollar amount of sales may yield much less insight than if the measurement process also includes actual sales performance in comparison to sales targets, sales to existing and new customers, revenue per sales transaction, sales performance for certain targeted products and services, costs of sales, customer satisfaction with the sales experience, and such other sales performance metrics as may be appropriate. If a company employs only a single measurement criterion, the indicated outcome can be highly distorted.

Relying upon a single, rather than multiplie, measurement criteria can be a mistake.

353 Negotiating Too Good of a Deal

In a business negotiation, the motivation usually is to get the very best deal possible. But sometimes, getting the very best deal may not be such a good deal, after all.

Sometimes in seeking to negotiate the very best deal, you can end up, at the end of the day, with no deal. If the deal that is negotiated, for whatever reason, results in the other side perceiving that it is not a reasonable, workable, equitable outcome, the other side may become unmotivated, even unwilling to do what is expected—or worse. The other side could either overtly or covertly sabotage the arrangement—or just choose not to play. If you negotiate too good of a deal, you may end up with no deal. The better course of action is to negotiate the optimal deal: good for you and good for the other side.

Negotiating too good of a deal can be a mistake.

354 Insisting on Being Reasonable

Some people, in approaching major business decisions—or any kind of activity for that matter—insist that others involved be "reasonable."

Great outcomes are sometimes achieved by being unreasonable. Indeed, insisting on being reasonable can be a guarantee of mediocrity. Some of the most successful leaders are extraordinarily successful because of being unreasonable—challenging convention, pushing people to do more than they thought was possible, confronting established norms. The unreasonable approach may prove to be more impactful than the reasonable approach.

To insist on being reasonable can be a mistake.

355 Emphasizing Being "A Nice Guy" Over Being Successful

Some people place more emphasis on being a nice guy than on being successful.

While many people would much rather interact with someone who is nice than abrasive, "niceness" does not necessarily contribute to superior competitive outcomes. Inevitably, conflicts arise between pursuing ambition and pursuing niceness. If a company's key people disproportionately favor the latter at the expense of the former, the company's performance will fall short of what it might desire. The company may lose market share and value, relative to competitors who place more emphasis on achieving results than on being well liked.

Emphasizing being "a nice guy" over the priority to achieve business results can be a mistake.

356 Unwillingness to Strain Key Relationships

If you are aggressive, competitive and ambitious, inevitably you are going to encounter possible conflicts between what you seek to accomplish and the desires of certain key relationships.

Some people may be uncomfortable with the intensity that successful performance involves. Some may favor cooperation and accommodation over competitiveness and dominance. Some may favor the "lower bar" approach, consistent with lower aspirations, than the "higher bar" approach associated with great ambitions. If you are aggressive, competitive and ambitious, inevitably you are going to face tension between what certain key relationships might want and what is necessary to accomplish what you want. If you favor what certain key relationships want, you may compromise what you want.

To accommodate others and to sacrifice the aggressive, competitive and ambitious style that accompanies outstanding business results, may be a mistake.

357 "Let Them Come to Us" Policy with Respect to Problems.

One approach to dealing with a prospective problem is to adopt a "let them come to us" policy.

The "let them come to us" policy means that the company takes a passive approach and presumes that if the other side has a problem, it will tell them about it. Unstated—but fundamental to this particular philosophy in dealing with problems—is the assumption that perhaps the other side will not recognize the problem, will be too busy to bring it up if they do recognize it, or perhaps will choose not to raise the problem, for whatever reason. The "let them come to us" policy is more passive and reactive than proactive and anticipating. Unspoken is the thought that "getting away with it" is somehow more important than the responsibility to the relationship. Although in the short-term the "let them come to us" policy can be rewarding, in the long-term it can be damaging, if not extremely negative.

To employ a "let them come to us" policy in dealing with prospective problems in key relationships can be a mistake.

358 Hoping That if You Don't Acknowledge a Problem it Will Go Away

Some companies and their leaders adopt a practice of ignoring problems in the hopes that the problems will go away.

Ignoring problems is an essential chapter out of the "what you don't know can't hurt you" book. This thinking is not too far removed from the strategy employed by the ostrich that sticks its head in the sand in the face of danger. The ostrich hopes that by the time it raises its head from the sand, the problem and danger will have disappeared. Maybe yes, maybe no. Companies that refuse to acknowledge problems—essentially adopting a stick-your-head-in-the-sand mentality in dealing with problems—do so at their peril. Although some problems will in fact go away, others problems, if not acknowledged, become only worse.

Failing to acknowledge a problem in the hope that it will go away can be a mistake.

359 Discounting the Importance of Emotional Intelligence

Effectiveness in the workplace calls upon many talents and resources. One of the most critical talents to be effective in the workplace is emotional intelligence.

Companies that emphasize the technical, at the expense of the emotional, do so at their peril. Notably, in an era of great technological advance, when arguably the *softer* skill aspects of workers' capabilities would be less prized, there has been an extraordinary groundswell interest in emotional intelligence. The field of emotional intelligence has gained great attention as companies more and more recognize that in periods of rapid change, which challenge conventional patterns, the crucial ability to cope with such change is often more emotional than technical. Similarly, in circumstances of accelerating complexity, as apply today, the critical capability to make sense of and integrate the complexity may be as much emotional as technical.

To place insufficient priority on emotional intelligence can be a mistake.

360 Presuming Tenure Equals Competence

In evaluating a company or its business unit, the role of tenure—how long people have functioned in particular positions—often is a priority consideration.

While tenure in a job can be a contributor to superior capability and performance, it does not guarantee these attributes. Merely because someone has been in a job for an extended period of time does not necessarily mean that that person is competent at doing that job. And merely because a person has had substantial experience in performing a function does not necessarily mean that person performs that function with competence. Tenure may, but does not necessarily, equal competence.

To think that tenure equals competence can be a mistake.

361 Too Much Emphasis on Unbalanced Evaluation Criteria

While employing multiple criteria to evaluate performance is usually better than employing a single criterion, it is important that there be balance among the different criteria employed.

In recent times, the concept of the *balanced scorecard* has gained significant interest. The balanced scorecard implies that multiple evaluation measures are employed and that there is an appropriate *balance* in the relative emphasis placed upon these measures. If too much emphasis is placed on one measure and too little on another—if the basis of scorekeeping is *unbalanced*—the outcome can be quite disruptive, if not extremely negative.

An unbalanced approach to performance assessment can be a mistake.

362 Treating All Employees Alike

Some companies have the idea that every employee should be treated the same as every other employee.

While equality, in many ways, is a very good thing, always treating every employee the same way is not necessarily good business. Some employees have the capacity to and actually do contribute much more to the company's success than do others. Often the employees who contribute the most work longer and harder, make the greatest sacrifices and undergo more hardships than do employees who have lesser commitment and make lesser contributions. If you treat the former the same way you treat the latter, you may find the former are less motivated to do what they do that creates so much value for the company. They may even be disinclined to continue to want to work with the company.

Baseball great Barry Bonds, who set the record for hitting 73 home runs in one season, and as of this writing is chasing Henry "Hank" Aaron's record for the most home runs hit in a career, is given special treatment by his team. In the San Francisco Giants locker room he has three lockers to the other players' single locker. He is provided a special reclining lounge chair. Further, Bonds is allowed to make decisions about what types of training and workouts he wishes to pursue. When the manager was questioned whether such special treatment was bad for the team's morale, the manager replied that any other player who could hit as many home runs as Barry Bonds and make such a contribution to the team's success could also be given three lockers, a special lounge chair recliner and anything else he wanted. The manager appropriately recognized that providing Barry Bonds with special treatment was the best thing for the team.

Treating all employees the same can be a mistake.

363 Concentrating on Upgrading the Weakest Performers

Business executives understandably want to improve the performance of the people in the organization.

In many companies, management's time is disproportionately directed to the problem people. This emphasis is understandable, for many leaders believe that they can turn a person around if only they expend enough attention, time and resources on the project. But is that really a worthwhile expenditure of resources? What is the impact, both on the overall company and on its objectives, of putting so much emphasis on a problem person at the expense of strong people, who, with perhaps a bit more guidance and assistance, could make exponentially greater contributions to the organization?

To expend disproportionate resources on problem people can be a mistake.

364 Thinking That People in Business Always Act Rationally, Reasonably and Responsibly

People in business are supposed to be rational, reasonable, and responsible—at least, that is the presumption.

Contrary to the textbook ideal of effective, efficient, and smooth operations, businesses sometimes proceed in ways that are more ineffective than effective, more inefficient than efficient, and more uneven than smooth. Rather than brilliance, company actions might reflect stupidity. Rather than championing integrity, duplicity and dishonesty can reign. Instead of competence, incompetence may rule the day. What is expected, logical, and desired does not always happen. As, in what has become a cliché joke, the airline flight attendant warning passengers, concerning the contents of overhead luggage containers, "shift happens."

Counting on business people always to act rationally, reasonably and responsibly is a mistake.

365 Concluding That if a Successful Result Is Not Achieved, the Problem Is That the People Did Not Try Hard Enough

When pursuing a new initiative and positive results are not immediately forthcoming, some may come to the conclusion that the people involved just did not work hard enough.

In pursuing a new initiative, hard work alone may not necessarily be the best course of action. If you are doing the wrong thing, no matter how hard you work at it, it won't make any difference. If something doesn't work, it is important to step back, assess the situation, identify the reasons, determine if corrective action needs to be taken, and then proceed.

Thinking that if something doesn't work, the reason is that the people didn't work hard enough, can be a mistake.

366 Thinking Years on the Job Is a Substitute for Knowledge and Legitimate Experience

Many people evaluate an individual's knowledge by how much experience that individual has. The assumption is that the more time someone has spent doing something, the more that person has learned—and therefore, the more competent that person is.

While experience can be a great teacher, if the experience is redundant and unchanging, little new may be learned. Once an interviewer asked a job candidate why he believed he was qualified. When the candidate replied that he had ten years of experience doing a similar job, the interviewer responded, "Yes, you have worked for ten years, but you do not have ten years of experience. You have one year's worth of experience, which you repeated ten times." The implication of this assessment was that the candidate really had not done anything significant, beyond what could be accomplished in one year.

Thinking that years on a job equates to experience and knowledge can be a mistake.

367 Tolerating People Who Are Only Out for Themselves

An organization serves multiple constituencies—shareholders, customers, employees, suppliers, securities analysts, investment managers, public officials, and more—each of whom have their own concerns, objectives and circumstances.

A manager who is excessively self-referential, concerned only with himself, rather than giving attention to outcomes for others, is much less effective than a manager who has a broader perspective. You cannot optimize and maximize your business outcomes if you tolerate a manager who fails to consider that shareholders, customers, employees, and others have needs that must be met.

Tolerating a manager who is more interested in his own outcome than the outcome of the company, shareholders, customers, employees and other stakeholders can be a mistake.

368 Failing to Deal with Non-Positive Feedback

As much as people might like everything to be milk and honey, sunshine and roses, the reality is that everything is not always positive.

A crucial strategic management attribute is the capacity to receive and deal with non-positive feedback. Executives who cannot constructively deal with non-positive feedback—who become defensive or perhaps appear graciously to take the non-positive feedback but then ignore it—are much less effective than those who can constructively deal with non-positive feedback.

It is a mistake for an organization to be led by people who cannot deal with non-positive feedback.

369 Refusing to Talk to Someone Who has Treated You Shabbily

Some people have the attitude that if a person treats them shabbily, they will have no more contact or interaction with that person.

There's a saying, "Fool me once, shame on you. Fool me twice, shame on me." If someone proves to be deceitful or dishonest, you have only yourself to blame, should you deal with him again and get cheated a second time. But sometimes it can be a mistake to cut off communications with someone on the grounds of past abuse. As renowned Dallas Cowboys owner Jerry Jones once observed, "If I stop talking to everyone who screwed me, I wouldn't have many folks to talk to."

Refusing to talk to someone who has been less than honest in dealing with you before, can be a mistake.

370 Failing to Address Integration After Merger

A successful merger involves not just the business and financial negotiations but also, and especially importantly, the subsequent integration of the business operations of the two companies. All the promised benefits of a merger will be lost, if insufficient and inadequate attention to integration is not addressed.

In the excitement of doing the merger, considerable attention is devoted to evaluating whether the merger makes good sense, gaining approval and buy-in of crucial stakeholders, addressing the financial implications, dealing with media relations, and reassuring nervous employees. But if the crucial tasks of integration—of systems, human resources, policies, organization, sales, operation, and technology—are not given sufficient attention, the promised benefits will not be realized. For those mergers that do not work, in the majority of instances the culprits are deficiencies in planning and weak execution.

If you fail to do the necessary merger integration planning and execution, you may make a mistake.

LEADERSHIP

371 Concentrating Political Capital on Politically Problematic Projects

Different projects have different levels of appeal to different audiences.

To get a project to go forward, you must recruit the involvement and endorsement of others. This recruiting is a political process, involving the expenditure of political capital. But if crucial influential people in the organization are opposed to a project, it may not be a good idea to expend resources to fight a losing battle or one that, if winnable, will exact a great price.

Pursuing a project that involves a too big a political price to achieve success is a mistake.

372 In Crisis Situation, Emphasizing Surviving More Than Thriving

In a crisis situation, it is more than natural to emphasize survival. After all, if the company does not survive, nothing else matters.

But it can be a mistake to put too much emphasis on surviving rather than thriving. If the leader does not focus on the longer term, on creating a vision of a better tomorrow, on making decisions today with tomorrow in mind, short-term choices may compromise long-term prospects.

To put so much emphasis on surviving that the longer-term priority of thriving is discounted can be a mistake.

373 Hiring a CEO from Outside the Company

When a CEO retires or is forced out, the board has to decide whether to hire the replacement from inside or outside the company.

Hiring the new CEO from outside the company can be the right decision, especially when there are no logical internal candidates and/or substantial change is needed. But sometimes hiring an executive from the outside is a mistake. If the company has a strong culture with established systems and procedures in place, an outsider may be more disruptive than productive. An outsider who fails to understand the company's culture may be less than productive in a leadership capacity.

Sometimes it can be a mistake to hire a CEO from the outside.

374 Jettisoning Corporate Memory

Corporate memory is the knowledge of what has come before in the company.

Corporate memory is valuable because it includes knowledge of prior key relationships, practices, market outcomes and interactions. If you have access to corporate memory, it can help answer a question or resolve a problem about something that happened some time ago. Corporate memory can aid in sustaining relationships that can lead to improved revenues and profits. Even if an executive's performance may be less than stellar, it may be appropriate to keep that person on the payroll because of the valuable corporate memory resource that person represents.

When a corporate house cleaning of troubled Tyco was implemented, the entire board and the top 50 executives were replaced. This decision certainly facilitated bringing fresh outlooks and perspectives to the business, but at what cost? What had been known about the past was now sacrificed. A better approach would have been to keep several key directors on an advisory/emeritus status, even though they might not vote in the board meetings. And a select number of executives could have been retained under some type of long-term contract, so that access to their knowledge and insights would not be lost.

Companies that are too quick to jettison corporate memory, getting rid of people who have been there a long time, but are perceived as less than the best contributors to the future, can be a mistake.

375 Underestimating True Cost of an Under-performing Senior Executive

When a senior executive under-performs, causing the company to deliver results below expectations, the cost can be extraordinary.

The costs of an under-performing senior executive extend beyond just failing to realize expected profits. Declining profits often mean lower stock price and higher borrowing costs, making it more expensive to get access to capital. When the under-performing senior executive is replaced, the cost can include an expensive "severance package," perhaps two or three times the annual compensation, plus the cost of recruiting a replacement, which costs can include search fees, relocation costs, and other charges, and can easily amount to the equivalent of a year plus of compensation. When a senior executive departs, the stock price may become more volatile and higher turnover on the board of directors may follow. The incoming new executive may want to bring in a new team, which can lead to replacing other executives. Adding it all up, the costs of an under-performing senior executive can be extraordinary.

Underestimating the true cost of an under-performing senior executive can be a mistake.

376 Selecting Technologist to Lead when Real Need Is Professional Management

When selecting leaders, company boards are often drawn to the idea of hiring a specialist in that company's basic business.

Boards at technology companies often seek a technologist to lead the company. If the company is facing fundamental technology challenges—if the core of what has to be addressed turns on technology—then a technologist may well be the best choice to lead the company. But if the underlying technology is sound, a technologist may not necessarily be the best choice to lead the company. The best choice may be a professional manager, whose portfolio of skills embraces leadership, strategy and management.

Selecting a technologist to lead the company, when the real need is for professional management, can be a mistake.

377 Failing To Share Credit

Recognition for great successes—in business or any number of endeavors—often is directed to a single person, when in fact many people are involved in achieving that success.

Although the Nobel Prize given for scientific discovery may be awarded to a single researcher, more often than not that researcher is supported by colleagues, a research laboratory, an administrator who took care of all of the details, laboratory assistants, financial contributors and any number of others. Same thing in a business situation. Although the spotlight may be concentrated on a single individual, as a practical matter many individuals are usually involved in achieving the success that is being recognized. Besides doing what is right, it is important to remember that if the recognition is not shared, the likelihood of repeating the success that commended that recognition in the future is diminished.

Not sharing credit for recognition of business success is a mistake.

378 Failing to Share Rewards

With success can come rewards. Arguably, the more success, the more rewards.

In some enterprises, the absolute amount of rewards that can be realized from a successful outcome can be extraordinary. But in all too many of these enterprises, the rewards may be disproportionately concentrated on a few, or even one, individual. The rewards are not shared. Will people who contribute to success, but do not get to share in the rewards, be motivated to continue to support that leadership and organization?

Companies that fail to share rewards do not build strong management teams to the same degree as do companies that share rewards. If a company fails to appropriately share rewards, it may find that those who contributed to achieving outstanding results are not inclined to work so hard the next time, or perhaps even to be part of the company.

Failing to share rewards with those who help create the success can be a mistake.

379 Asking People to Work for you but Failing to Honor Their Contributions

Some executives expect their people to work hard for them, but then they do not respect the work that they ask their people to do.

In bicycle racing, the team leader is supported by *domestiques*—riders who set the pace, break the wind, carry food and drink, and sacrifice their own individual chances so that the team leader can triumph. Notably, the smart team leader splits the winning prize money evenly among all the *domestiques,* recognizing that although he may cross the line first, it is the team who helped him get there. Team leaders who fail to respect their *domestiques* may not fare so well in the next race.

Asking people to work for you but failing to respect the work that they do is a mistake.

380 Failing to Pay Sufficient Attention to the Most Important People

In most organizations a small number of people disproportionately influence what happens in that organization.

Savvy executives know the importance of identifying the people who are the most important, by virtue of their power, the respect they command, and their ability to make a difference in what happens in that organization. If the most important people are ignored, the chances of getting outstanding results are diminished. By identifying and interacting appropriately with the most important people, the prospects of superior outcomes are meaningfully enhanced.

Failing to identify and work effectively with the most important people can be a mistake.

381 Emphasizing Generalized Cheerleading Rather Than Specifics

Many managers recognize that positive communications and feedback to employees can motivate better performance.

However, encouragement and generalized cheerleading are much less impactful than specific, particular comments. Most people respond much better to a message that relates directly to them than to a message that could be applied to anyone. Further, most people respond better to a message that recognizes and acknowledges specific actions and contributions, rather than some generalized comment.

Being too generalized in communicating with people can be a mistake.

382 Inconsistent Messages

Leaders who deliver a consistent message are more likely to achieve results than those whose messages are inconsistent.

More can be accomplished at work when the workflow is continuous and uninterrupted, than when it proceeds in start, stop, redirect, restart fashion. Think of riding a bicycle. If you ride consistently, you will get to your destination faster and with much less effort than if you are continually stopping, expending effort to reduce your momentum, and then starting up again, expending more effort to gain momentum. A consistent, purposeful approach achieves better results than does a start-and-stop-and-restart approach.

Delivering inconsistent messages can be a mistake.

383 Imposing Corporate Policy on Field Offices

Corporate policy imposed on field offices should be congruent with and derivative of the realities in the field.

Too often, people at corporate headquarters come up with policies that may, on the surface, be appealing, but which, when subjected to examination, may be inappropriate. What works at corporate headquarters may not work in the field. As a case in point, consider dress code. The more formal business attire that is appropriate in a major business center may not be appropriate in a more relaxed, suburban setting. Insisting that employees in field offices located in a more relaxed, suburban setting, dress according to corporate standards appropriate to a major business center could lead to depressed morale or even undesired turnover. The policy that is appropriate for headquarters may not be appropriate for field offices.

Imposing corporate headquarter policy in field offices can be a mistake.

384 Imposing the Culture of the Acquiring Company on the Acquired Company

When a company acquires another company, there is the question of how to address cultural differences.

Some acquiring companies have the idea that their culture should dominate. Such thinking can lead to making decisions that may not only diminish the value of the acquired company but also dramatically damage it. One time a company acquired another whose sales force worked from their homes. The acquirer's requirement that all sales people show up and work at the office every day caused the vast majority of them to leave the company. Cultural insensitivity can have a big price.

It can be a mistake for an acquiring company to insist on imposing its culture on the acquired company.

385 Holding Convictions but Not Communicating Them

Strong business leaders have strong convictions.

As important as strong convictions are, if those convictions are not effectively communicated, they are no more useful than weak convictions or no convictions at all. If a leader's convictions are not effectively communicated to the appropriate audiences, then the prospect of that leader being successful is rather remote. An effective leader not only has strong convictions, but effectively communicates those convictions.

It is a mistake to have convictions but not communicate them effectively.

386 Failing to Deal with People as People

As companies expand in scale, certain tasks that earlier were adjuncts to a manager's job may become established as separate jobs unto themselves. As a consequence, interactions that previously occurred in the course of the regular business day are replaced by a formalized human resources function.

As important as it is to provide the benefits of economy and power that can result from a larger scale organization in administering certain human resources functions, it can be a perilous proposition if the company loses touch with treating people *as people.* If the human resources function becomes too automated, too systematized and too streamlined, the personal aspect of treating people *as people* may be lost. If people feel they are viewed more as cogs in the larger machine than as individuals, their loyalty and commitment will be compromised and the company will suffer.

Failing to deal with people *as people* is a mistake.

387 Relying upon the Wrong Type of People

Strategy ultimately comes down to people assessment.

No matter how good your strategy, if you do not have the right people in place to implement it, you cannot be successful. If a manager makes appropriate assessments of people, the prospects of the enterprise achieving its objectives are meaningfully enhanced, than if the manager's assessment of people is less than prescient. Crucial to business success is to avoid placing too much reliance on the wrong types of people.

Placing too much reliance upon the wrong types of people can be a mistake.

388 Labeling Bullying Behavior as Principled Unreasonableness

There can be a subtle distinction between principled unreasonableness—the initiative that can achieve great results against all odds—and negative behavior that is no more than bullying, manipulation or exploitation.

Some bullies may justify their manipulative and exploitative conduct by saying that they are "unreasonable," in the same way that certain great executives who accomplish great things are "unreasonable." But this type of unreasonableness is very different than principled unreasonableness, where integrity and respect characterize personal interactions. Masking bullying behavior with a misapplication of "unreasonable" compromises the organization's ultimate effectiveness.

Justifying bullying, manipulative and exploitative conduct as principled unreasonableness, when in fact it is not, is a mistake.

389 Too Many *Yes Men*

The majority of powerful people are very confident in their own convictions and do not like to be contradicted.

In many instances, powerful leaders will attract a group of staff and line executives who may be more oriented to keeping that powerful person happy than to telling that powerful person what he may really need to hear. Rather than saying "no" to what is asked, be it an assignment or opinion about a new idea, these individuals say "yes." But if a company is overly dominated by *yes men*, the company may suffer, by saying "yes" to a decision, when the appropriate answer really is "no."

Too many yes men can be a mistake.

390 Rationalizing/Justifying Consistently High Turnover

Organizational turnover, resulting from people not staying in their job for any sustained period of time, can compromise the enterprise's productivity and effectiveness.

If people do not stay in their job for a period of time, organizational memory is lost and customer relationships are more difficult to sustain. If the organization does not perceive, chooses to ignore, or perhaps somehow rationalizes or justifies consistently high turnover, the ability of the organization to be effective is inherently compromised. If the organization is unable or unwilling to address the implications and consequences of turnover, it will not do nearly as well as if those causes and consequences can be confronted and addressed.

Rationalizing or justifying consistently high turnover is a mistake.

391 Excessive Reliance on One Employee

Companies that rely excessively on one employee put themselves at inappropriate risk.

If you depend too greatly on one particular employee's skill, availability, initiative, and energy to get things done, you have exposed the business to inappropriate, needless, and unnecessary risk. The business may perform superbly as long as that employee is available, motivated, and able to work. However, in the event that the employee becomes unavailable, is disinclined or unable to work, then the business may be brought to a standstill.

Exclusive reliance upon one employee is a mistake.

392 Paying Out Too Much Profits as Compensation

One of the biggest mistakes companies can make is to pay out too much of their profits as compensation.

If a company pays too much of its profits in compensation, then the company is compromising its future and cheating its shareholders. Some years ago the Salomon Brothers partnership sold their firm to Philbro. After a while, it turned out that Salomon, despite having public shareholders, was still paying out a substantial amount—as much as 75%—of its profits as bonus compensation to employees. Employees were making way too much money, relative to their market value and the contributions they were making, and the shareholders were being shorted.

Paying out too much of your profits as compensation is a mistake.

393 Relying on Superstars Rather Than Systems and Structures

Some companies decide that the way to obtain outstanding results is to hire superstars.

While superstars can make extraordinary contributions to a company's success, a superstar strategy can be very risky. What if the superstars leave? What if the superstars demand ransom as a condition for staying? Better to invest in systems and structure, so that the company can be effective without relying on superstars. Then, if you can add superstars to operate within the system's structure, you can do even better. But if you have to choose, systems and structure is by far the preferred way to go, over the superstar route.

Relying on superstars over systems and structures can be a mistake.

394 Pay Before Performance

Many management theorists assert that performance and compensation should be linked.

The intention behind linking performance and compensation is that compensation will both reward and motivate performance. If performance is delivered but not compensated, people may become unmotivated to repeat that performance, or choose to leave the company. But if you pay before performance is delivered, you may find that the motivation to deliver the performance is less acute than if pay were contingent upon the performance being delivered.

Pay before performance can be a mistake.

395 Emphasizing Perks Only for Executives

In some companies very attractive, even lavish packages of "perks"—"perquisites", the good things that are included in a compensation package other than the paycheck—may be provided for executives.

If a company places too much emphasis on perks for executives, the company may be in for trouble. Executives may develop an over-inflated opinion of their worth, presuming that the perks are entitlements rather than something that must be earned and justified by strong performance. Other employees, who work hard and support the success of the company but do not receive such lavish packages of perks, may become disenchanted and resentful. Excessively lavish perks for executives is not a good business practice.

Companies that emphasize perks only for executives are making a mistake.

396 Lacking a Coach

While some extraordinary performers achieve high standards without having a coach, this outcome is the exception rather than the rule.

A coach can add a great deal to an athlete's performance. A coach can motivate an athlete to achieve beyond what he or she might think is possible. A coach can push an athlete to work harder than the athlete might have wished to work. And a coach can inform the athlete when it is better to back off than to push ahead. Just as any competitive athlete limits his or her potential by not having a coach, so, too, does an executive constrain his or her prospects for success by refusing to work with a coach.

Lacking a coach can be a mistake.

397 Not Coachable

Some people are inherently non-coachable.

When top sports teams look to select players, they favor those athletes that are coachable. Being coachable means being receptive to coaching—to receiving guidance and feedback on performance, accepting third party review, and listening to and learning from criticism. The best athletes, the best performing artists, and the best executives are coachable. Those athletes, performing artists and executives who are coachable will outperform those who are not.

A coachable person is open to guidance, support, and assistance. Coachability is not necessarily related to a person's talent or excellence. Some of the most talented people, however, are the most coachable, for one of the reasons they are so talented is that they are so receptive to realizing the benefits of effective coaching. People who are uncoachable—not open to coaching—are going to be much less successful than those that are. If a company has too many people that are uncoachable, it cannot be effective.

Resistance to coaching is a mistake.

398 Believing Effective Coaching Is Based on Experience

Whereas coaching was once primarily considered in the context of athletic performance, more and more coaching is viewed in the context of business and organizational performance.

Some people involved in coaching in the business setting have what might be described as quaint or outmoded ideas as to what coaching involves. One high profile executive proclaims he coaches those in his company when he interacts with people one-on-one, and when he is spending time with groups of people. This executive's philosophy of coaching is simply to impart his experience, proclaiming that what he has to offer is valuable, "not because I'm so smart but because I have seen it one hundred plus times."

Without diminishing the reality that this executive may have some interesting and relevant experience to impart to others, to think that coaching is merely passing on lessons learned from experience is a misunderstanding about what coaching is all about. While experience may enhance the effectiveness of a coach, much more important than experience is knowledge, the capacity to adapt that knowledge to the particular individual or situation at hand, and the capacity to motivate the individual to achieve high levels of performance.

To think that effective coaching is basically about passing on your experience is a mistake.

399 Afraid of Hurting Feelings

Some companies hold off on making important decisions because they are afraid of hurting feelings.

While sensitivity to feelings is important, it is not so important that significant decisions should be postponed, delayed or not made on a timely basis. Life is not necessarily always peaches and cream, sunshine and light, milk and honey. Not everyone can always get what he or she wants, when they want it, how they want it. Companies who can't move ahead to take care of business—on the grounds that they don't want to hurt anyone's feelings—will lose ground to those that do move ahead.

Not wanting to hurt people's feelings can be a mistake.

400 Ambiguity Regarding How an Employee Would Fit into the Larger Picture

Although some companies operate from the thinking that an employee needs to be nothing more than a "cog in the wheel," other companies emphasize having employees understand their role in the larger picture of the enterprise.

When an employee understands his or her role, that employee is in a better position to make effective contributions to the company. A sense of the larger purpose can motivate superior performance and enable an employee to make more informed decisions. When employees know how what they do fits into the larger view of the company, those employees can be more effective.

Ambiguity concerning how employees' tasks fit into the big picture of the business can be a mistake.

401 Ignoring People's Lives Outside of the Office

Some executives have the attitude that they should have no involvement in people's lives outside of the office.

While there are good reasons for drawing certain boundaries between what happens in the office and what happens in the personal lives of employees outside of the office, to ignore what happens to people's lives outside of the office can compromise the organization's effectiveness. By understanding some of the pressures people are going through in their outside-the-office lives, the company may have a better understanding of reasons behind performance on the job. The more the company can do to be understanding of and supportive of people's lives outside of the office, the more likely those people are to perform at a high level when they are at the office.

Ignoring people's lives outside of the office can be a mistake.

402 People Not Happy

A company in which people are not happy—a condition that characterizes all too many organizations—is unrewarding for both the people and the company.

When people are not happy, they are not likely to be as productive as if they are. If people are not happy, your customers will pick up on it and those customers will be less likely to continue to patronize the business. If people are not happy, they will not make as effective decisions as if they were. If people are not happy, the company will not be nearly as effective as it could be.

An unhappy-people approach to business is a mistake.

403 People Don't Like Their Work

If people do not like their work, they are unlikely to be as effective in their work as if they do like it.

Some studies have said that as many as 75 percent of people do not like their work. How rewarding is it to lead people who don't like what they are doing? How rewarding is it to work with people who don't like what they are doing? How rewarding is it to be served by people who don't like what they are doing?

A company dominated by people who don't like their work is making a mistake.

404 Failing To Invest in Training

In an economy that is more and more characterized by knowledge, information, and specialized expertise, companies recognize that people need training to be effective and competitive.

Unless companies provide support for people to develop their knowledge and skills, those people will likely not have access to the training and professional development they need. When people rely on outmoded knowledge and dated skills, their effectiveness in their work will necessarily be compromised.

Companies that fail to invest in training can never create lasting shareholder franchise value that creates true enduring company worth, beyond the most recent operating period. For example, many real estate brokerage companies pay out most of their revenues and profits as compensation to brokers, rather than investing in training. The brokers who work for these companies have more limited knowledge and professional capabilities, than had investments been made in their training.

Failing to invest in training is a mistake.

405 No Economic Rationale to Invest in Training

Some companies take the position that they do not wish to invest any resources in training their people.

Many arguments may be advanced for not investing in training. Some managers reason that people are so busy and have so much to do, that the company cannot justify the time away from their job responsibilities for training. Or they think that it would be a waste of resources to invest in training, because what if the people they trained left after the training? The company would have spent all the money on training but not gotten the benefit.

Inevitably, if a company spends money on training, some of the investments it makes in training people who leave will not be realized. But what if the company did not spend the money to train people and those people actually stayed? Surely, the company would have saved the money that it would have otherwise spent on training, but the company would also forego the benefits it would realize from having invested in training.

Believing there is no economic rationale to invest in training can be a mistake.

406 Failing To Invest in Systems

Companies that fail to invest in systems cannot create lasting shareholder franchise value. Systems, either manual or automated, provide consistency, promote efficiency, enhance production and reduce costs.

Companies that do not invest in systems are too dependent on the skills, productivity and inclinations of particular people. If those people leave, the company's ability to get the work done is dramatically diminished. As long as the company has not provided valuable business platforms with appropriate systems, the company cannot realistically command much profit; therefore, such companies have limited value.

Failing to invest in systems is a mistake.

407 Failing to Have Appropriate Systems to Support Your Business

Basic to delivering efficient, consistent, economical products and services are sound systems.

Every business should be built on a foundation of systems. Systems include procedures, processes and automated means of doing certain tasks. These systems enable employees to do their jobs more effectively and to serve customers more responsively. Systems are needed in all relevant areas of the business. Indeed, superior businesses have systems to create, manage, and enhance other systems.

Managing a business without systems can be a mistake.

408 Compromising Effectiveness and Efficacy of System by Buying Unbundled, Uncoordinated Solutions

A company may determine that it can address a particular strategic objective through a system solution, but then, through faulty implementation, not get the results it needs.

Consider a retail store that has decided to improve its profitability by better matching its purchasing with inventory and customer purchasing patterns. The company decides to buy and implement an automated customer purchase database and inventory management system. So far, so good. But if, in the implementation, the company chooses different, separated and uncoordinated suppliers of the computer software and hardware, the installation, the initial data loading, and the training, then troubleshooting and servicing the system may be very problematic.

To choose a collection of unbundled and uncoordinated suppliers for component parts of an important system, instead of an integrated performance-guaranteed solution from a single vendor, can be a mistake.

409 Inability to Stick with a System

Research has proven that the right system, steadfastly adhered to, can produce outstanding results.

Even though people may understand it is important to have the right system, in practice all too many managers do not adhere to a system. Perhaps they find it too monotonous, get bored, and drift off to more interesting and more rewarding tasks. But those managers who have the self-discipline to stay with the system can prosper at the expense of those who do not.

Failing to adhere to the system can be a mistake.

410 Failing to Employ Planning and Systems to Achieve Lower Costs

Effective planning and systems can meaningfully reduce costs.

Consider the example of a technology company that previously handled all customer inquiries in the field, at a cost of $50 per customer inquiry. By centralizing the customer inquiries, the cost was reduced to $20 per inquiry. And because the centralized approach could provide a higher level of service, with better support and training, only half the number of calls were required to resolve a particular issue. Whereas before it would take an average of two communications to resolve a customer's problem, now problems could be resolved in a single communication. As a consequence, the cost per customer inquiry fell from $100 to $20, a savings of 80%. With some 2,500 inquiries per month, the company saved $200,000 per month—or nearly two and one-half million dollars per year.

Operating a function at too high of a cost by failing to employ planning and systems is a mistake.

411 Failing to Understand That Technologies Can Be Used to Advantage

One of the fundamental challenges of business is that the senior executives, who make the decisions about major capital commitments to technologies, generally know much less about those technologies than others in the organization.

The dual forces of dramatic advances in the power of technology, and the growing influence of technology in every aspect of society, challenge senior executives to confront decisions that their predecessors never addressed. Whereas technology once was a minor factor for a majority of businesses, today it looms as the second or third largest expense category for most enterprises—just after employee compensation costs, and sometimes larger than facilities costs.

While some executives have substantial background and training in technology, most do not. Consequently, many executives are challenged to make decisions about technologies that may be more *black box* than crystal clear. If executives do not take the time to learn what they need to know and if senior technology managers do not help their colleagues learn what they need to know, the company will be at a fundamental disadvantage.

If executives do not know enough about technology to make informed decisions about their company's technology expenditures, it can be a mistake.

412 Uncoordinated Business and Technology

Technology is supposed to serve a business, not operate independently of it.

If there is not close, even seamless, alignment between the business and the technology employed to support that business, the prospects of the technology making a meaningful contribution to the company achieving its objectives are compromised. Business operations and the associated technologies to support those business operations need to be carefully and closely aligned.

If business and technology are not closely aligned, it can be a mistake.

413 Technology as an End in Itself

Technology is supposed to be a means to a desired outcome, not the end in itself.

Companies that approach technology as an end in itself—becoming overly involved in the sophistication of the system, its latest features, and its cutting edge capabilities—are concentrating on the wrong thing. The thing you should concentrate on is how technology helps to achieve the desired end. Technology is a means, not the end.

Viewing technology as the end, rather than the means to achieving the desired end, can be a mistake.

414 Separating Technology and Business Culture

Technology is often thought of as a hardheaded digital enterprise, while culture is a softer discipline. Consequently, when approaching corporate strategy, many do not readily link technology and culture.

Although technology and culture are each significant domains, when the two are aligned, business productivity can be much greater than when they are separated. No technology project proceeds in a vacuum, for the very approach to technology implementation carries cultural connotations concerning whether decision making is centralized or distributed, whether information access is open or closed, and the relative role of empowerment and communication within the organization. Notably, in assessing new project initiatives, astute executives rate intangible factors—access, incentives, culture, innovation, empowerment, communication, people issues—at least as important as hard quantitative ROI (return-on-investment) measures.

Approaching technology and culture as separate, independent elements of business can be a mistake.

415 Too Much Focus on Uniformity, Control and Standardization

Many businesses understandably emphasize uniformity, control and standardization.

The essence of automating processes is to develop an approach that can be used repetitively, over and over and over, thereby achieving uniformity and control. In many instances, uniformity, control and standardization are central to realizing outstanding outcomes. But in some instances, too much focus on uniformity, control and standardization can compromise customization, block creativity, and frustrate customer service. In those instances, the benefits such standardization are not justified by the costs.

Placing too much focus on uniformity, control and standardization can be a mistake.

416 Too Little Focus on Uniformity, Control and Standardization

Contemporary culture encourages individuality, creativity and innovation.

One consequence of the emphasis on individuality, creativity and innovation is to downplay standardization. Many seem to think it is a binary proposition—you are either one or the other, but not both. In the quest for individuality, some organizations end up with too little focus on uniformity, control and standardization, and the enterprise's productivity may suffer.

Too little focus on uniformity, control and standardization is a mistake.

417 Overlooking Benefits of Individualization for Customers

In dealing with customers, companies need to balance the economy and control advantages of automation with the important priority of considering that each customer is an individual with unique needs, circumstances and requirements.

Businesses that pay too little attention to their customers' individual circumstances do so at their peril. Company processes and systems that are insufficiently capable of recognizing and accommodating the need for individualized approaches—because they put excessive emphasis on uniformity—may find their customer relationships suffer. As important as uniformity and automation are, if there's too little individualization in the company's offer—if its products and services are indistinguishable from another company—less than positive outcomes may ensue.

Ignoring the benefits of individualization is a mistake.

418 Thinking because E-mail Is Electronic, It Is of Less Consequence Than Written Documentation

The Internet has stimulated a proliferation of communications that differ from traditional verbal conversation and paper documents.

Many of us communicate via the Internet in ways that differ markedly from how we talk and how we might write a business letter or memorandum. Some of these communications are less precise, less thoughtful, or less considered than a business letter or memorandum might be. Some do not recognize the possible consequences associated with this different communications style, while others excuse their more informal, less precise approach with the observation that because the communication is electronic, it is not really different from speech. The thinking is that the standard of accountability that applies to a verbal communication is a lesser standard than that applying to written communication. But as some companies are learning, to their chagrin and regret, e-mail communications can be retained, retrieved, and replayed, often in embarrassing, incriminating, and expensive ways.

To think there is no accountability associated with electronic communications is a mistake.

419 Thinking E-business Is a Fad

Some people no longer consider that e-business is important.

Because electronic business got so much media attention in the later 1990s and into 2000, and then a few years later was no longer the dominating, all-consuming front-page news story, it is tempting to dismiss e-business as a once-but-no-longer-popular fad. But it would be a real mistake to think that e-commerce is a candidate for hula-hoop status. E-business is a powerful development that cannot be ignored. To do so is to put your enterprise at risk.

Thinking that e-business is a fad is a mistake.

420 Thinking That the Internet Is Everything

With all of the popularity and interest in the Internet, many have concluded the Internet is all that matters.

Certainly, the Internet is extremely important and matters a great deal. But the Internet is not the only thing that matters. To emphasize the Internet at the expense of other important themes and trends in business is shortsighted. To do so runs the risk of not having the necessary context and broader view that are necessary to channel properly the Internet's capabilities.

Thinking that the Internet is the only thing that matters is a mistake.

421 Thinking Business Basics do Not Apply to Internet Business

Because the Internet is so revolutionary, some believe that it calls for new business practices.

Since the Internet has revolutionized established business models, some Internet enthusiasts assert that business practices should also be revolutionized, with the thinking that new models need entirely new business principles. While some established old business practices have no role in Internet business, some business basics—such as meeting customer needs by providing valuable goods and services, making a profit, and managing cash flow—are very relevant. The Internet does not obsolete business basics.

Thinking that the basics of business do not apply on the Internet is a mistake.

HOW YOU CAN AVOID MISTAKES

HOW YOU CAN AVOID MISTAKES

Your very desire to avoid mistakes makes mistakes much less likely to occur. If it is your intention to avoid mistakes, this intention will go far in ensuring better outcomes than if you paid little or no attention to avoiding mistakes.

But beyond the intention to avoid mistakes, there are a number of powerful and specific things you can do to ensure fewer mistakes. Among the particular approaches you can take are:

- Comprehending what a mistake is and is not.
- Considering how your dreams and aspirations may influence the outcome you seek.
- Emphasizing character—ultimately what you do is a reflection of your character.
- Applying consciously and positively the sequence of first thinking, next deciding, and then acting.
- Engaging proactively and purposefully in appropriate planning and preparation.
- Using appropriate decision-making models, processes and resources.
- Applying relevant and useful criteria and standards.
- Identifying and validating assumptions, plus confirming information relevance and accuracy.

- Questioning everything that is associated with what you are thinking of doing.
- Undertaking the relevant investigations to confirm the reliability of representations and to uncover crucial facts and influencing forces.
- Recognizing the powerful role of perspective in how you frame and approach a situation.
- Addressing explicitly the significant role of personal style and emotional factors in influencing outcomes.
- Understanding the deal and what's at stake.
- Employing strategic thinking.
- Considering the profound implications of time and place.
- Involving family and stakeholders' perspectives to guide your contemplated decision or action.
- Effectively accessing and utilizing, to your best advantage, multiple people resources.
- Imaginatively employing the perspectives of prominent persons.
- Perceiving what games you are playing and understanding how the rules are applied.
- Engaging in lifelong learning to improve your knowledge and capabilities.

- Acknowledging the inevitability of change and adversity, plus proactively responding to the opportunities that these forces offer.

Each of these approaches is discussed more fully below.

In the book *How You Can Make Better Decisions To Avoid Mistakes—the 731 Keys,* numerous specific techniques, tactics, approaches, guidelines and more are presented for each of these twenty-one categories of keys to avoiding mistakes. Additionally, many hundreds of quotations are included that provide extra perspective, insight, depth and inspiration to guide you to avoid mistakes. The commentaries that follow are summaries and encapsulations of 731 keys from this book.

1. Understanding What a Mistake Is—And Is Not

Arthur Wellesley, the first Duke of Wellington, emphatically stated, "*There is no mistake; there has been no mistake; and there shall be no mistake,*" which assertion he perhaps underscored with his defeat of Napoleon Bonaparte at Waterloo. Napoleon himself—who perhaps made mistakes at Waterloo—believed that mistakes are pervasive, as he proclaimed, "*He that makes war without many mistakes has not made war very long.*"

In spite of Wellington's assertion, mistakes do pervade every aspect and every arena of life. But even though mistakes are part of life, many can be avoided.

Understanding what a mistake is—and is not—is basic to avoiding making mistakes. The range and breadth of the dictionary definitions of the word "mistake" is instructive:

- Wrong action
- Wrong statement
- Erroneous action or statement, following from faulty judgment
- Erroneous action, following from inadequate knowledge
- Misunderstanding of implications
- Misunderstanding of meaning of something

- Blunder in a choice made about something
- To make a wrong judgment
- To be wrong

Etymologically, the word "mistake" refers to a wrong or erroneous "take"—a miss-take—an incorrect take on a situation.

Fundamentally, a mistake results from erroneous *thinking, deciding* and/or *acting*. While many who think about mistakes might tend to emphasize erroneous action—reflecting deficient implementation of what you have decided to do—focus on action alone is insufficient, especially if the action follows from deficient thinking or erroneous decisions.

It is crucial to recognize that "mistake" refers not merely to miscalculation in the implementation of action but also, significantly, to an *input* to the process of decision making that precedes and is the basis for action. A mistake is not a wrong or unwanted outcome. Rather, a mistake is the input—the thoughts, decisions, and actions that lead to the outcome, not the outcome itself. *Inputs* are controllable, while *outcomes* are susceptible to influence, but not necessarily to control. While some outcomes may certainly be controllable, many are influenced by others' decisions and actions—over which you have no control—as well as by uncertain events and random circumstances. Avoiding mistakes involves addressing the inputs—the thinking, decisions and actions—that can lead to error.

2. Dreams and Aspirations—Your Rainbow

George Bernard Shaw said, "*You see things and you say, 'why'? But I dream things that never were, and I say, 'why not?'*"

The closer and more energetically you can embrace and engage the spirit of "why not?" the more likely you are to embark on a path that will avoid mistakes and be true to your aspirations, dreams and desires. The more you diverge from a path that is true to your aspirations, dreams and desires, the more likely you are to make mistakes. If anything you contemplate doing is in conflict with or in contradiction to what you want to achieve in your life, to what you want your life to be, and to what you want to realize and accomplish, chances are you will make mistakes.

It is important to consider explicitly your aspirations and dreams for your life. Ask yourself whether what you propose to do advances your aspirations. What is the downside of what you propose to do in terms of your aspirations? Might the outcome compromise your ultimate aspirations? Is the action you contemplate informed and influenced more by others' priorities or does it truly reflect your priorities? Does what you contemplate doing support what you really want?

Resources you devote to anything that is not congruent with your life purpose will inevitably diminish the resources available for those involvements that *do* promote your life purpose. This is an excellent standard to test whether something you are considering doing will be a mistake or not. If you aim for the very best, you are more likely to avoid a mistake than if your aim is not so high. As

W. Somerset Maugham so wisely observed, "*It's a funny thing about life; if you refuse to accept anything but the best, you very often get it.*"

3. Character—It's Up To You

Mistakes can occur when you act in ways that do not promote—or that compromise or even that directly contradict—your values and beliefs. Everything you do in life is ultimately a statement about who you are as a person and who you aspire to be. The most effective personal character standard is to consider whether what you are thinking about doing is something you choose to take responsibility for, without blaming anyone else, no matter what the outcome. This attitude of responsibility for self is captured by sportswriter Gary Smith's insight, *"A great fighter's a man alone on a path. He must feel that he is a maker, not the made. He must feel that he has fathered himself."*

Your thoughts, decisions and actions are the manifestations of your character, your values and your beliefs. Your thoughts, decisions and actions also reflect your attitudes and the strategies you employ in how you approach life, how you experience life, and how you confront and respond to adversity.

To develop your character and your ability to take responsibility for your actions is to decrease the number of mistakes in your life. As the *Dhammapada*, the ancient Buddhist text, states, *"One person on the battlefield conquers an army of 1,000. The other person conquers himself. The second person is greater."* The more aware you are of your values, beliefs and attitudes, the less likely you are to commit mistakes.

Is what you are contemplating doing compatible with your underlying values? Does it reinforce or contradict your values? Does it reflect integrity and correspond with your personal code of conduct? Is it true to yourself, and not the result of what someone else would do or would think you should do? How does what you are thinking about doing reflect your responsibility to the present, as well as to past and future generations?

As contemporary Indian teacher Swami Muktananda observed, *"Everything depends on one's attitude and understanding...that is why it does not matter where you are, or where you live, but rather who you are and what your inner state happens to be."*

4. Thinking, Deciding, Acting —Cool, Calm, Collected

Mistakes result from a shortfall or breakdown or some other deficiency associated with thinking, deciding and acting. When the sequence of think, decide, act is reversed—if people act first and only later consider the decision and then the thinking behind the decision—a mistake is more likely to result, than if action follows from a decision that is preceded by thought.

In marksmanship, the discipline is first to get ready to shoot, then aim the weapon, then fire the weapon. This same ready-aim-fire sequence applies to the sequence of thinking about what you want to do, then deciding to do it, and then acting. One of the most powerful ways to avoid mistakes is to confirm that the thinking, analysis and reflection that are the basis of decisions are likely to lead to positive outcomes as opposed to mistakes.

Logically, if an outcome reflects competent implementation of a decision, which decision follows from the thought that precedes that decision, then any resulting mistake is the result of deficient thinking. How you think can influence what you do, even if you do not consciously connect your actions to the thoughts that precede them. Nevertheless, by explicitly considering the ways and means and approaches to thinking about a decision, you improve your chances of avoiding mistakes.

Included among the many different facets or aspects of thinking are investigating, planning and preparation, learning, questioning assumptions and making use of different perspectives. At the same time, it is important to remember that thinking alone may not, in itself, be sufficient. Recognizing our dependence on factors over which we have little control, Werner von Braun said, "*We can lick gravity, but sometimes the paperwork is overwhelming.*"

In thinking about the decisions you might make, it is important to distinguish *deciding* from thinking and from action. The better a job you can do in effectively and sequentially applying thinking, deciding and acting, the less likely you are to make mistakes. As Johann Wolfgang von Goethe noted, "*Nothing is more terrible than ignorance in action.*"

5. Planning and Preparation —Being Ahead of the Game

Business guru and author Michael Gerber recognizes the importance of planning and preparation in a business context when he notes, "*Businesses that are planned are more successful than those that are not. Businesses that change their plans on an ongoing basis are more successful than those whose plans are static.*" In any context, appropriate planning and preparation are crucially important to avoiding mistakes and having successful outcomes.

Planning and preparation are central to avoiding mistakes. Former Secretary of State Henry Kissinger famously observed, in response to a question concerning how he had time for thinking about all of the very complex, difficult decisions that he faced, "*In this job, there is no time for thinking. You must decide on the basis of thinking already done.*" Planning and preparation allow you to be in a position so that your thinking is "already done."

Every decision ultimately reflects the implementation of a plan, which may be explicit but more often is implicit. Good planning and preparation are the predecessors for and the means to achieve good outcomes, for as Lewis Bendele said, "*A man without a plan for the day is lost before he starts.*" It has been shown that *writing down a plan*, making it explicit on paper, greatly increases the likelihood of its effective implementation. It has been accurately said that *it's not a plan until you write it down.* Then, once you have a plan, it is important to adhere to it, for those who *plan their work and work their plan* are more likely to achieve success and avoid mistakes, than are those who neither engage in planning nor implement the plans they make.

The decision or action you contemplate can be written or drawn as a flow chart that identifies in sequence the key steps along the way. Such a method is helpful in breaking down the decision or action into small steps. Sun Tzu, the ancient Chinese military strategist, advised *"Plan for what is difficult while it is easy. Do what is great while it is small. The most difficult things in the world must be done while they are still easy. The greatest things in the world must be done while they are still small. For this reason, sages never do what is great, and this is why they can achieve greatness."*

In making a plan, identify what elements of the path are most critical. Devoting proportionately more resources to and concentrating more attention on what is most critical increases the likelihood of a successful result. Plan several moves ahead. The most effective board game and card players think ahead, considering what the likely play will be several moves in advance. They also consider what the other players might do or what cards might be dealt, and plan what action to take. Another technique is to describe all the possible problems of what you are proposing to do. Then list all the reasons to do the exact *opposite* of what you plan. Such a process can lead to unexpected insights.

6. Decision Making : Models, Resources and Processes —Tools to Use

Decision-making is the process by which thought is translated into action. Every action—or inaction—follows from a decision, for as theologian Harvey Cox has most cogently observed, "*Not to decide is to decide.*"

Every decision involves the application, sometimes explicitly but most often implicitly, of models, rules, decision tools and processes. The decision models employed and the decision techniques utilized in implementing the models have a big impact on whether the decision results in a mistake. As international consultant and statistician W. Edwards Deming asserted, "*There is no such thing as bad people, just bad systems.*" The more knowledgeable you are about various models, decision tools, rules, processes and their applications, and the more skilled you are in applying them, the more likely you are to avoid mistakes.

In approaching a decision, the degree of conviction, confidence, and adherence or challenge to convention can exert a powerful influence upon whether or not a mistake is made. Decisions that follow from strong and well-justified confidence may be expected to result in better outcomes than those in which such confidence is lacking. Because ultimate certainty is seldom achievable, understanding the requisite level of conviction as a *precondition* to a go-ahead decision can be an important way to avoiding mistakes. And, considering what you are thinking of doing in relationship to convention—how adhering to or challenging convention may influence the likelihood of the outcome—can exert no small influence upon avoiding mistakes.

Decision-making is a skill that can be developed through any number of study and self-development approaches. You can improve your decision-making ability by a conscientious program of professional development. Such a decision-making professional development program might include self-directed study, reading, college courses, seminars and workshops, participation in a study group, keeping a decision-making journal, and consulting with specialists in decision-making.

You improve your chances of avoiding mistakes by increasing your knowledge and skills in applying decision-making competencies. Reading books about decision-making can give you a wealth of decision-making tools and methodologies. Because management textbooks can provide insights to help you make better decisions, read textbooks that cover the disciplines relevant to the decision, and the industry that is the context for the decision. Constantly be in search of new perspectives, information, points of view, and ways of looking at things. Be avaricious in your consumption of information.

The richer your background of decision-making knowledge, the greater your skills in applying that knowledge, and the more useful information that you gather before making a decision, the more likely you are to avoid mistakes. The more aware you can be as to how the decisions involve the process by which thought is translated into action, the greater likelihood you have of your avoiding mistakes.

7. Criteria and Standards—You're the Judge

Decisions ultimately involve the application of criteria. The sharper and more expansive your thinking in regard to the criteria that you employ in making decisions and making choices, the more likely those decisions and choices will be ones that avoid mistakes.

Sometimes people may be implicit, vague or general about what their decision criteria and standards are. This very vagueness, in itself, is a statement that their criteria and standards are general rather than precise. A very different emphasis was employed by Ted Williams, one of the greatest hitters ever to play baseball, who insisted on explicit standards when he observed, *"If I swung outside of the strike zone, then how would I know where to draw the line?"* The less precise you are, the more likely you may be to make a mistake. The more particular and thoughtful you can be about your decision criteria and decision standards, the more exacting the frame of reference you have to employ in assessing whether a decision is a good one...and the more likely you are to avoid mistakes.

The very process of thinking about your decision criteria can lead to avoiding making a mistake. You might wish to consider whether your criteria are specific or universal, implicit or explicit, situational or generalizable, conventional or iconoclastic. Further, decision criteria that might work in a mature, established situation might be much less relevant for a nascent, emerging situation. And, decision criteria may be different depending upon cultural considerations and especially geography. The decision criteria that are right in one place may be inappropriate, illegal, or even dangerous in another place.

In applying criteria and standards it is useful to consider that the relevant criteria for yesterday may not be the relevant criteria for today and especially for tomorrow. Learning theoretician Donald Schon conveyed the essence of this notion when he stated, *"Any idea in good currency is no longer appropriate to its situation."*

8. Assumptions and Information

Perhaps the most important key to avoiding mistakes is to challenge assumptions and verify the accuracy of information. All too many mistakes are traceable to reliance upon assumptions about some aspect of the decision or action that have little or no connection with reality. Had the assumptions been subjected to scrutiny before the decision was made or the action was taken, deficiencies would have been revealed or their inaccuracy and/or unreliability would have been discovered.

One of the most famously inaccurate assumptions was made by Ken Olsen when he asked, "*Why would anyone want a computer in their home?*" At the time, he was the head of Digital Equipment Corporation, then the largest minicomputer company in the world. Of course, he was not the first person to misperceive the potential of computing technology and information processing. In 1957, the editor in charge of business books for Prentice Hall remarked, "*I have traveled the length and breadth of this country and talked with the best people, and I can assure you that data processing is a fad that won't last out the year.*" And consider Thomas Watson, the man who initially grew IBM, who asserted, "*I think there is a world market for maybe five computers.*"

Whether you make a mistake may often turn on the degree to which the assumptions turn out to be reliably actionable or prove to be unreliable for making significant decisions. Your decision is also based upon combinations of reliable information and information whose reliability is less than certain. One of the most important ways to avoid mistakes is to check, verify, and confirm the information and data behind your assumptions. At the end of the day, these considerations of fact/information and assumption/less-than-certain information ultimately inform what you elect to do.

You can put your assumptions to the test by looking at what would happen if the validity of the assumptions on which your decision and action are based proved to be invalid. How would the invalidity of critical assumptions influence the decision and action that you are contemplating? What can you do to confirm the validity of these assumptions?

9. Questioning—The Means to the Answer

A questioning approach to avoiding mistakes considers *what* you need to know, how much of what you need to know you *already* know, and what you do *not yet* know. Such inquiry can lead to insights that can be crucial to avoiding mistakes. As St. Jerome wrote in the fourth century, "*It is worse still to be ignorant of your ignorance.*" By probing for insight into the underlying logic, rather than merely accepting what is first presented or considered, you can improve the chances of avoiding mistakes.

Some very good ways to avoid mistakes are to check twice, apply deeper analysis, analyze again, double check what was done, engage in second guessing, take a second look, then look deeper and review the entire decision process one more time.

Ask questions, of yourself and others. Question the motives and influences of others involved, especially those whose representations or actions you are relying on. If what you contemplate doing depends upon competent execution, then question the competency of the persons responsible for that execution—even if it's yourself.

Ask yourself what the most important question is that should be asked about what you plan to do. What questions are you avoiding? Ask yourself what questions you hope no one asks you about this decision. And inquire as to what questions you should have asked, but didn't.

Questioning others, questioning authority, even questioning yourself, is not always easy. The question, after all, can be perceived as a challenge, if not to one's own knowledge then to the reliability and veracity of another's representations. But as uncomfortable as raising a question may be, be mindful of the admonition that the only inappropriate, or even stupid question is the one that is not asked.

And never forget to ask yourself the question that Colombo might ask, if he were talking to you. Colombo, the television detective played by actor Peter Falk, was renowned for asking a probing, seemingly unrelated question at the conclusion of an interview, just as he left the room. This apparently unrelated question sometimes elicited the critical information he was seeking.

What is the significant—but unasked—question, which answer might illuminate insights about your contemplated action?

10. Investigations—Sleuthing for Success

Investigation involves going beyond the obvious, to look for the fundamental causes of why something happens. As Ben Franklin tellingly observes concerning fundamental causes, "*For want of a nail, the shoe was lost. For want of a shoe, the horse was lost; for want of a horse, the rider was lost; for want of a rider, the battle was lost; for want of a battle, the kingdom was lost.*"

Many mistakes result from decisions made on the basis of faulty facts, deficient data, unreliable information, and ineffective input. To make good decisions, you need good data and reliable information. Investigations can both verify data and also confirm the reliability and relevance of information. In implementing investigations, how one marshals such considerations as applying multiple intelligence, obligations, disclosure and checklists can, incrementally and especially interdependently, have a major influence on avoiding mistakes.

In pursuing your investigations, it is important to keep in mind the inherent relationships between what comes before and what comes after, what is above and what is below, what is the source of influence and what is influenced. America's foremost authority on the game of bridge, Ely Culbertson, noted, "*A deck of cards is built like the purest of hierarchies, with every card a master to those below it, a lackey to those above it.*" Recognizing structural hierarchy and its implications can be a key to avoiding mistakes.

Although sometime the indicated course of action is immediately obvious, in other instances investigation is a necessary precondition to an effective decision. Investigation is necessary to uncover the substance behind the representation, to dig below the surface, to differentiate the truth from the fiction. As Aesop so wisely observed, "*Appearances often are deceiving.*" While many recognize that *perception* is important, few may explicitly consider just how important differentiating perception from reality can be in avoiding mistakes. Investigations can be crucial to avoiding mistakes by revealing the degree to which what is learned through investigation matches what was initially perccived.

The capacity to distinguish between causation and correlation is also crucial to avoiding mistakes. Without investigation of source causes, it is all too easy to make a mistake by confusingly concluding that coincident correlation is true causation.

Investigation is useful not only to gather what you need to know to make an informed decision and to guide the actions you contemplate taking, but investigation can also be very helpful in confirming what you have already decided to do. Investigation of the underlying premises, facts and theories can often lead to an illuminating insight that can make all the difference. As Mark Van Dorn astutely noted, "*An unexamined idea, to paraphrase Socrates, is not worth having; and a society whose ideas are never explored for possible error may eventually find its foundations insecure.*"

11. Perspectives—If I Could See What You See

While many recognize that perspective is important, few may explicitly consider just how influential it can be in avoiding mistakes. The importance of perspective is made clear in Archimedes's famous statement: "*Give me a place to stand, and I will move the earth.*" Different perspectives can lead to very different decisions and therefore to very different outcomes. Sometimes a crucial consideration in whether a mistake is made or not is the vantage point that is applied to the decision.

As important as other perspectives can be in avoiding mistakes, too seldom are they brought to bear. In fact, thinking about things in new, even unconventional ways, is far more uncommon than common. As Kent Ruth observed, "*Men can live without air for a few minutes, without water for two weeks, without food for about two months—and without a new thought for years on end.*"

Different perspectives can lead to insights that can be the key to avoiding a mistake. In applying different perspectives, it is helpful to keep in mind that often the more challenging and more controversial a perspective, the more useful it may be, especially if your objective is to avoid a mistake. For as George Seldes said, "*All ideas are controversial, or have been at one time.*" With this in mind, if you were to apply a challenging perspective to your decision, might you think about it differently? Perhaps, before committing to a major course of action, you might want to read a book whose author's premises, ideas and values are very challenging to those that you hold.

Decisions are typically approached in the vocabulary and perspective of the discipline that is most familiar to the decision-maker or the decision issue. Thus, decisions concerning financial commitments are viewed from a financial perspective. Decisions involving organizational issues are evaluated from a human resources perspective. But how might the decision appear if a different disciplinary perspective were brought to bear?

By stepping away from your decision and employing a different perspective, perhaps hypothetical or imagined, you can bring a range of insights to see things that you might not otherwise have seen. And, in so doing, you can avoid a mistake that you might otherwise have made. To this end, Peter M. Suschak said, *"All of us are watchers—of television, of time clocks, of traffic on the freeway—but few are observers. Everyone is looking, not many are seeing."*

The power of perspective is illuminated by a trenchant observation of *Star Treks'* Spock, played by Leonard Nimoy. Spock asked perhaps the ultimate perspective question when he said, *"I find the question 'Why are we here?' typically human. I'd suggest 'Are we here?' would be the more logical choice."*

12. Personal Style and Emotional Factors

Although many business textbooks would tell you that a decision is good or bad in general, in reality decisions are much more personal and unique to the enterprise and people involved, than generalizable to all companies and all individuals, regardless of their circumstances, mindsets, and ways of being. A decision that might work for one company or organization or person at one time, might not work for others at another time, or in different circumstances.

In approaching decisions it is helpful to be aware of different personal styles and emotional factors that you might be bringing to the decision process. By considering explicitly the role of such personal and emotional factors, insights may emerge that can enable you to avoid mistakes.

Optimism properly applied can be the key to avoiding a mistake. As former San Francisco Mayor Willie Brown observed, "*It is absolutely necessary to be optimistic! Optimism is the only way to go when things are tough and rough.*" But if optimism is improperly applied, optimism can be a contributor to a mistake. Sometimes a touch of pessimism is more useful than too much optimism. In this regard, legendary investor Philip Carret said, "*I am always turned off by an overly optimistic letter from the President in the annual report. If his letter is mildly pessimistic, to me that is a good sign.*"

It is not so simple as to say one should have a particular emotional approach; rather, awareness of one's own style and approach is the key to understanding and avoiding mistakes.

Since many mistakes are partly attributable to personal, emotional factors, rather than to shortfalls in decision-making skills, the more advanced your personal development and self-awareness, the less likely you are to make mistakes. Among the many approaches to personal development and awareness are workshops and seminars, counseling, working with a personal coach, self-directed study and reading, journaling, meditation, prayer, and other spiritual or religious practices.

As noted above, a decision you make or an action you take should fundamentally be consistent with your dreams and aspirations as well as with your values and beliefs. It is also wise to take into account your personal tendencies, your "way of being." Are you a decisive person? If you tend to be indecisive, what might your decision be if you were more decisive? Do you have a positive mind or a pessimistic mind? Is your plan built upon a positive or pessimistic view of the future? Are you overly cautious? What is your tolerance for an adverse outcome? For ambiguity?

Being aware of the large role that personal style and emotional factors can play in the process of thinking-deciding-acting can help you avoid mistakes.

13. The Deal and What's at Stake

Although some actions and decisions have nothing to do with deal-making and deal terms, many, in fact, do. To avoid mistakes, it can be helpful to consider the situation from a deal-making perspective, including explicitly assessing the situation and what your expectations are in the situation. The better you can understand the implications of the stakes involved, the more likely you are to avoid a mistake.

Decisions and actions can vary dramatically in terms of their stakes, payoffs, possibilities and risks. The difference in magnitude of what is involved in a deal was captured well by former Seagram CEO Edgar Bronfman's observation, *"To turn $100 into $110 is work. To turn $100 million into $110 million is inevitable."* As the prospects for gain and the relative size of that gain may vary dramatically with scale, comprehension of how scale influences the odds of realizing a desired outcome can be an important consideration in avoiding a mistake.

If you take for granted the stakes that might be involved and the associated risks, you may find that you elect a course of action that is very different than what you would choose, were you to engage in more explicit, considered assessment. All too often, people make mistakes when they are implicit rather than explicit about the risks and the stakes involved.

You need to understand the deal, not just from your perspective, but from others' perspectives. Ask questions: What is at stake here? What is the upside potential and the downside exposure? Is there an appropriate match between what is at stake in this decision and the resources you have applied to the decision? Does the "deal" reflect terms that are good for you? Is it sufficiently rewarding, not only for you but for others? How can you make the deal better for you and for others? Is there a way that you could modify the proposed decision or action to make it more joyful and fun?

It can be helpful to view the decision in terms of a bet. Is this a bet you would want to make? Would you "bet the ranch" on this decision? To improve the odds of the bet, what role might insurance, assurance, and guarantees play? To confirm that you are carefully considering what is really at risk, consider employing a devil's advocate perspective—if the devil were in control, what would the devil favor in terms of the outcome of your contemplated decision?

Since many mistakes are attributable to miscalculations, concentrating on calculation appropriateness and accuracy is an important means of avoiding mistakes. Always check and recheck the numbers. Under pressure of getting a lot done in a short period of time, it's easy for numbers to be transposed or some other rudimentary arithmetic error to creep in. In a situation where the numbers are important, it can be helpful to have a third party check the numbers. And, remember that numbers can both reveal and conceal, as Erin Levenstein recognized with the observation, "*Statistics are like a bikini. What they reveal is suggestive, but what they conceal is vital.*"

Calculations are usually linked to value. Value, in turn, is connected to *expectations* of value and *perceptions* of worth. Where money is involved, it can be a good idea to consider the expectations and perceptions of others involved in the deal. At the same time, you should not be so concerned with the others' deal that you lose sight of your own perspective on the deal, for as legendary real estate developer William Zeckendorf instructed, *"Don't worry about my deal. Worry about whether the deal is good for you."*

14. Strategic Thinking— Creativity Counts

Mistakes are more likely with an inferior strategy and less likely with a superior strategy. Superior strategic thinking leads to clarity, insight and substantiation. Superior strategic thinking considers systems interdependencies and explores reasons, meaning and implications. The capacity to think strategically about alternative courses of action and to probe their implications and consequences leads to better decisions than if such capacity were lacking.

Basic to strategic thinking is what journalists refer to as the five "W's and "H." Rudyard Kipling expressed this when he wrote:

> *"I keep six honest serving men*
> *They taught me all I know.*
> *Their names are:*
> *What and Why and When and How and Where and Who."*

Central to a superior strategy is clarity. The greater the clarity that can be brought to a strategy, the greater the likelihood of avoiding mistakes. Does your strategy reflect clarity in terms of the logic of your decision? Consider the logical flow of your contemplated decision. If you proceed, logically, step-by-step, to connect all of the dots, what do you learn? Is there any element that has a less logical justification than other elements?

A strategic approach explicitly considers the participants' strengths and weaknesses as well as the opportunities and threats to the involved individuals and enterprises. Decisions and actions that play to strengths are more likely to be successful than those that do not. Decisions that insufficiently consider weaknesses are more likely to result in a mistake. Decisions that exploit opportunities are more likely to lead to positive outcomes, just as those that insufficiently consider threats are likely to lead to mistakes.

The ability to extend thinking beyond normal boundaries—to think both out of the box and in different boxes—is an important strategy skill. Being able to appreciate the interdependencies of multiple factors that can influence outcomes is a crucial strategy skill that, effectively applied, reduces mistakes.

An important strategic management tool is the "critical success factor" concept—those parts of the plan whose successful accomplishment are critical to the overall positive outcome. To avoid mistakes, it is important not just to examine the assumptions, but also to identify the critical success factors that are a precondition to a successful outcome. What are the critical success factors for your proposed venture? The more you can identify, comprehend, and confirm critical success factors, the more likely you are to avoid a mistake.

15. Time and Place—Where and When?

One of the most important resources that should be considered to avoid mistakes is time. Time exists in the context of place and space. But as important as time and place relationships are, they are seldom sufficiently considered. As eighteenth century English essayist Charles Lamb insightfully noted, "*Nothing is more important than space and time—yet nothing is less important, because I never think of them.*"

By considering explicitly time and its relationships to place, you can improve your chances of avoiding mistakes. What works and is appropriate and rewarding at one time and place, may not be at another time and place. Similarly, what can be frustrating, unachievable and disappointing at a certain time and place, may change entirely to be enjoyable, doable and rewarding, if the time and place are different. How do time and place influence what you are doing?

If you are in the right place—physically, figuratively, emotionally, spiritually, cognitively and in every way—you are more likely to make good decisions. One of the most empowering acts that you can take to enhance your outcomes and avoid mistakes is to do what you need to do to be in the right place. Equally important to the right place is the right time. But time is dynamic, not static. As Samuel Taylor Coleridge wrote, "*In today already walks tomorrow.*" By thinking in different time frames—back in time and into the future—you improve your chances of avoiding mistakes.

By being conscious of and understanding the role of timing and how different results can ensue at different times, you can avoid mistakes that you might otherwise make. What may be right for one time may be wrong for another time. What might be right for one place might be wrong for another place. What could be right for one relationship at one time and place could be totally wrong for another relationship at another time and place.

Time and place can be utilized in many ways to avoid mistakes. For example, when faced with a decision, turn your attention and involvement to something else for awhile, and then come back to the contemplated decision/action, to discover if time away might illuminate how you might consider things. It can be very helpful to take a walk, which provides a moving, low energy, active meditation process. On your walk insights may arise that can assist you. By taking some time away from your active daily schedule, you may find that a *quiet mind* offers insights that might not otherwise emerge.

Consider how timing might impact your decision. Sometimes, people get everything right but still make a mistake because their timing is wrong. Is this the right time for what you propose to do? If you had more time to make the decision, would you make the same decision? If not, why not? What does that mean for the decision you are contemplating?

The importance of time is captured well in Arnold Weinstein's observation, "*We write in time. We write against time. We write to capture time.*"

16. Family and Stakeholders' Perspectives—The Bigger Picture

Decisions informed by multiple perspectives are better than those informed by limited perspectives. While multiple perspectives do not guarantee avoidance of mistakes—after all, some of the most colossal mistakes result from collective group think and mass myopia—effectively involving multiple perspectives can meaningfully improve decision outcomes. Often, the perspectives of your family and others who have a stake in the decision can be very illuminating.

Every decision or action involves multiple stakeholders, many of whom may not initially appear to be so obvious. The process of involving everyone who has a stake or perceives they have a stake in a decision increases the likelihood of those stakeholders feeling good about the decision *process*—even though they might not necessarily like the decision *outcome*. The more you can explicitly recognize that others have a stake in what you are doing, and the more you consider what you are contemplating from their perspectives, the more likely you will be to avoid mistakes. As Japanese executive Ken Hayashibara insightfully observes, "*If the person is over 40, I tell him he should do something because it is good for Japan, good for the company, good for his family and finally good for him. If the person is under 40, I tell him he should do it because, first it is good for him, good for his family, good for the company, and finally good for Japan.*"

You might ask yourself who could be impacted by the decision and action that you contemplate. The numbers and kinds of people with a stake in what you do is often far greater than you might initially recognize. How can you expand your horizons to consider all the people who might have a stake in what you plan to do? Many of the people that are impacted by your decision will never know about it. If they were to know, how would they feel about you? How would you feel about their remarks? Who will benefit from the decision and action you propose? Who might lose?

The viewpoints of family members and others close to you can often be illuminating. Would your family be proud of what you propose to do? Why or why not? What would your partner or spouse say about the decision you are contemplating? You may wish to ask them directly—or you may wish to ask them in your mind—and take note of what they say. If you were to ask your son(s) or daughter(s) about the decision, what might they suggest to you? If you do not have a son or daughter, what might your niece or nephew or some other child close to you say about the decision you are thinking about making? If you were to ask your parent for advice about this decision, what might your parent say?

Involving others, especially those who have a stake in what is to be done, is crucial to avoiding mistakes. By bringing in the viewpoint of those who have stewardship responsibilities, who have a stake in the outcome, as well as those who are observers, you can improve the chances of getting the desired results. The wisdom of this approach is clear in former President Lyndon B. Johnson's observation, "*There are no problems we cannot solve together and very few we can solve by ourselves.*" The perspectives of others can meaningfully improve the likelihood of avoiding mistakes.

17. People Resources—There's Help Everywhere

Outcomes are influenced by accessing and effectively using people resources. The mere process of interacting with people and explaining your decision—telling them what you plan to do, soliciting their involvement, asking for their help—can improve your decisions and reduce the likelihood of you making a mistake. The contributions that people can make to improving an outcome is captured well by marketing innovator William Bernbach's statement, *"An idea can turn to dust or magic, depending on the talent that rubs against it."*

Help is available from people in any number of forms. You might ask others whether they would recommend that you get help for the decision you are about to make. You might decide to retain a consultant or work with a personal coach.

In seeking help from friends, coaches, devils' advocates, futurists, historians, logicians, attorneys, and so on, you might want to get input in person, or you might want to get it hypothetically, considering what they might say to you about your decision, were you to consult with them.

What if, for example, a prosecuting attorney were to review what you were about to do, with the objective of finding holes in it, exposing its vulnerability and tearing apart the logic—what might that prosecuting attorney tell you? If a competent, fair judge were to review everything and to reach a judgment as to whether what you are trying to do is appropriate, likely, proper, and wise—what verdict might that judge render? If an investigative journalist were to probe behind the scenes, talking to all the people involved and reviewing all the documents—what might that investigative journalist discover and reveal? What could a logician tell you about the internal consistency of what you plan to do?

You might go to an Internet chat room and describe generally what you have in mind, in a way that will not compromise any confidential information, to discover if you encounter any interesting ideas or insights. There are numerous services available on the Internet through which experts (sometimes self-fashioned) offer their advice and counsel on any number of topics. Perhaps there is an Internet expert source that relates to your decision, from which you could gain some insights to help you make a better decision.

You could even consult a magician—if a magician could wave a wand to make a magic outcome for your proposed venture, what would that outcome be? Where is the "magic" most needed? Other less conventional but helpful approaches could be to consult the *I Ching* or a handwriting expert or a Tarot reading. The results may be startling and illuminating.

In considering the position insisted upon by a challenging person, it is helpful to consider that those perspectives which challenge traditional, conventional approaches and ways of being are often much more useful and productive than those that merely reiterate or endorse the conventional way. After all, a mistake is more likely to be avoided by challenge than by endorsement. As cultural anthropologist Angeles Arrien advises, *"Bless those who challenge us. For they are insisting on our growth."*

18. Prominent Person's Perspectives

Thinking about what you contemplate doing from the perspective of a prominent person can be a key to avoiding mistakes. This is not to say that prominent people do not make mistakes. To the contrary—some of the most extraordinary mistakes are made by the most prominent people. Some people become prominent, notoriously so, *because* of the mistakes they make.

However, considering what you are thinking of doing from the perspective of a prominent person, particularly a person of inspirational or pivotal importance to you, can be helpful. The very prominence that differentiates them from others causes them to be more visible, more influential and more memorable than others. Their strongest features, magnified beyond the norm, make them larger than life. By modeling what you most admire or respect in a prominent person, you may avoid a course of action that might otherwise be a mistake.

What if you were to approach your decision from the perspective of a great person such as Jesus, Buddha, Gandhi, Confucius, Winston Churchill, or some other great person? What if you were to ask if Ms. Manners would approve? What about considering if a highly regarded management theorist such as Peter Drucker would endorse your action? Could consulting such legendary fictional detectives as Sherlock Holmes and Miss Marple help you avoid mistakes?

What other people can you think of, whose perspectives are especially meaningful and significant to you? Could their perspective help you avoid a mistake?

19. Perceiving What Game You Are Playing and How the Rules are Applied

Another perspective on mistakes is to consider that virtually everything you seek to accomplish can be thought of in terms of its being a game—one that involves yourself at a minimum, and usually involves others as well. One of the most devastating causes of mistakes is a lack of understanding as to what game is being played, what the rules of the game are, how the rules are applied, what influences outcomes, and how one wins the game. In one sense, a mistake can be thought of as losing the game.

In many instances, the fundamental mistake is that people do not recognize that they are playing a game. It is basic to recognize that you are playing a game, for often others may involve you in something that you do not initially recognize as a game. The game may be routine and familiar, or new and unknown. The more you understand the game and how it is played, the better you can play it and the more likely you are to avoid a mistake. Recognizing that every game is a learning opportunity, you can apply the teaching of Aristophanes that *"The wise learn many things from their foes."*

Does the game involve yourself alone or are others involved? If others are involved, what is your relationship to them? Are others opponents or collaborators? Perhaps your relationships shift over time. In considering the games you may play it is important to reflect whether it is a game in which there are clear winners or clear losers, or might there be numerous winners and losers? What are the rules of the game? Further, what are the games within the game? As a case in point, the Tour de France bicycle race is a game of multiple games: a race between individuals and between teams, races for time and races for points, races for sprinting and races for climbing, races that are solo time trials and a team time trial, races for a single stage, and ultimately a race to win the race overall.

For any game you are playing it is important to understand what outcome you seek. Addressing what outcome you seek necessarily follows from understanding why you are playing the game. Do you choose to play this game or are you forced to play this game by others? Do you play the game joyfully and volitionally—or are you involved in the game reluctantly and defensively? Is not playing the game feasible or even preferred to playing the game?

What outcomes do others seek? How do their desires influence the outcome you seek? Legendary former Green Bay Packers football coach Vince Lombardi said, *"Anything is possible if you are willing to pay the price."* What price are you willing to pay?

It is important to determine whether the game is a zero sum game—where one player's gain is at the expense of another's—or whether it involves the possibility of more than one winner. What is rewarded in this game? Does it favor competence? Hard work? Expertise? Connections? Seniority? Merit? What is the role of chance in influencing the outcome?

At the most basic level, you need to consider whether the game you are playing is decided on the basis of your standards, or someone else's standards, or independent standards. What are the rules and who decides? As Stanley Garn tellingly observed, *"If the Aborigine drafted an IQ test, all of Western Civilization would presumably flunk it."*

The award-winning movie *A Beautiful Mind* dramatized the life of John Nash, who was awarded the Nobel Prize in Economics for his pioneering work in applying the theory of games to decisions. Game theory is a powerful discipline that can aid your understanding of games and support your crafting superior ways to play games. While game theory can not eliminate adverse outcomes, it can meaningfully reduce the chance of your making a mistake.

20. Learning—It Is Lifelong

People with more learning and understanding are less likely to make mistakes than those who have less learning and understanding. The more you study and learn, the more likely you are to avoid mistakes. Those who pursue learning as a lifelong endeavor are more likely to avoid mistakes than those who do not. Renowned investor and philanthropist John Templeton remarked, *"It's only common sense to study success, not only in investments, but in all facets of life."*

The importance of learning as a path to avoiding mistakes was brought home by Renaissance thinker Michel deMontaigne when he said, *"Nothing is so firmly believed as what we least know."* If you would avoid mistakes, you continue to learn—perhaps especially in those areas where you already possess significant knowledge.

How can you enhance the effectiveness of your knowledge acquisition? The most important factor is having a philosophy of continuing to learn, no matter what the circumstances. As Eugene S. Wilson observed, *"Only the curious will learn and only the resolute overcome the obstacles to learning. The quest quotient has always excited me more than the intelligence quotient."* It has been said that the most important objective of an effective college education is not to teach the contents of a curriculum as much as it is to teach the students to be self-educating. As Henry Ford said, *"Anyone who stops learning is old, whether at 20 or 80. Anyone who keeps learning stays young. The greatest thing in life is to keep your mind young."*

As you proceed with any adventure or activity, you have the opportunity to learn as you go, and not only from your own experience and mistakes. Although theory and principles may sometimes appear to be abstract and remote from the real world, much in the realm of theory and principles is very relevant and useful. One way to think about theory and principles is that they reflect conceptual decision rules that can be adapted and applied to any number of situations. Further, by reading about and paying attention to others' mistakes, you can gain exposure to what can go wrong and thereby be more sensitive in making your own decisions. The lessons you learn can be applied to your present and future activities.

Keeping a journal can be a most effective means of self-directed personal work, and can lead to improvements in many aspects of your life. Through keeping a journal you can gain insights into and greater clarity concerning your life. In particular, keeping a journal of your decisions—what they are, how you made them, how they turned out, what you learned, what you would do differently or do the same the next time—can improve your decision-making abilities. One approach is to keep a *mistakes* journal—as contrasted to a more general *decisions* journal—in which you might record lessons learned from mistakes made. The very act of identifying and recording lessons learned can be of immense value.

The more skills you have in decision-making competencies—which skills can be gained through any number of study and self-development approaches—the more likely you are to avoid mistakes. By going beyond just *gathering* experience to *considering lessons* that can be learned from that experience, you can meaningfully reduce your chances of making mistakes. And by extending your study beyond just your own experience into considering the experience of others' mistakes, you can further improve your odds of not making mistakes.

21. Change and Adversity—Constant and Inevitable

Change and adversity are inevitable. As Heraclitus so sagely noted, "*You cannot step twice into the same river; for other waters are ever flowing onto you.*" The quest for a positive outcome inevitably involves risk. Economist Milton Friedman said, "*The more we go out on a limb, the more fruit we find, since the most fruit is at the end of the limb.*" Recognizing that the quest for more fruit involves going out on a limb, it is helpful, in seeking to avoid a mistake, to consider the risks and take the initiative to deal with those risks.

Change can be both positive and negative, relatively and absolutely, and at different points in time. What might at first appear to be a major setback, can, ultimately, emerge to be extraordinarily positive. What seems initially to be a setback may evolve to be an opportunity. And, contrarily, positive initial changes may, over time, have less than positive implications for others.

Sometimes the first approach is the best and only good approach. But usually by revising, fiddling, tinkering, and fine-tuning, the approach can be improved and ways found to avoid mistakes. Since rapid change is ever more prevalent in the world today, considering what you are contemplating doing in the context of what might change and how it might change can help you avoid mistakes. By carefully considering what could happen to throw a monkey wrench into what you plan to do, you can increase the likelihood of avoiding mistakes.

Norman Cousins observed, "*Wisdom consists of the anticipation of consequences.*" The essence of avoiding mistakes, and thereby achieving a positive outcome, is the anticipation of consequences. But anticipating consequences is a daunting undertaking, for as Bill Gates noted, "*People tend to overestimate how much things will change in the short term, but really underestimate how much things will change in the long term.*"

Major confrontations are often determined by the different levels of tolerance that different parties have to deal with possible adverse consequences. Adversity, after all, is inevitable. For as Dolly Parton noted, "*If you want the rainbow, you've got to put up with the rain.*" Those who have a greater capacity to cope with adversity will be more likely to avoid mistakes in the long term. Similarly, those who are able to be more immune to criticism, and to potentially damaging consequences, are more likely to avoid mistakes.

The process of avoiding mistakes is continual, ongoing, never ending. It is not something in which you can get to a point in life where you can confidently presume you will never make a mistake. As advertising great Mary Wells Lawrence observed about the business of advertising, "*In this business, you can never wash the dinner dishes and say they are done. You have to keep doing them constantly.*" So, too, to avoid mistakes you have to keep doing it constantly.

* * *

You can learn more about how to avoid mistakes in ***How You Can Make Better Decisions to Avoid Mistakes—the 731 Keys,*** which contains 731 specific proven techniques and hundreds of quotations that can provide you a different, illuminating, provocative, even challenging perspective.

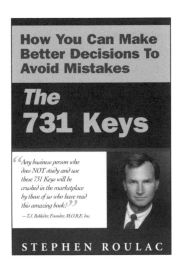

Afterword

My objective in *421 Business Strategy Mistakes* is to provide a meaningful chronicle of important mistakes that can occur, from both a large, big-picture perspective as well as a more detailed, micro point of view.

Any listing of mistakes such as those in this volume, however, should properly be thought of as a beginning, rather than a final, comprehensive listing. Strategy is a broad topic, and a book such as this cannot realistically cover all of the mistakes that would be relevant to the many aspects of this subject. A savvy, experienced professional who specializes in a particular aspect of business could prospectively think of many more mistakes in the area of his or her particular specialization.

While the table of contents provides a general categorization of mistakes, the process of creating this book did not start with listing of categories and then thinking of mistakes under those categories. Rather, once the collection of mistakes had been prepared, a categorization to provide some order and structure was established. What started as a small list of mistakes evolved to a boatload of mistakes, more or less randomly generated, which were then organized into what could be considered an imperfect categorization.

Depending upon reader interest, future books might follow that expand on business strategy that are under-covered here or that address entire new categories of mistakes. I invite you to contribute to this ongoing process. Among of the ways you might contribute are:

1. Suggest a better categorization of the mistakes concerning business strategy. What categorization would you suggest?
2. What more mistakes concerning business strategy can you think of? What are the missing mistakes?
3. What is your best story about a mistake?

We have it on reliable authority that doing one or more of the above is reputed to be a good way to deal with any consequences of waking up in the middle of the night with mistakes on the brain.

To make this more interesting, each quarter, so long as interest justifies, we will recognize the most useful and relevant categorization scheme, the most significant contribution of new mistakes, and/or the most intriguing, provocative/illuminating story about a memorable mistake, by offering a $100 gift certificate that may be used for any Property Press books and information products.

You can suggest your mistakes categorization, tell us about missing mistakes, or regale us with your most memorable mistakes story by going to www.propertypress.com (click on Mistakes), or sending a fax to Mistakes at 415-451-4343, or writing to Mistakes, 709 5th Avenue, San Rafael, CA 94901.

Acknowledgements

421 Strategy Mistakes and How You Can Avoid Them reflects what I have learned in observing, studying, researching, practicing, working as an advisor to, and interacting with thousands of executives, professionals, advisors, investors, consultants, athletes, coaches, and others over the last three plus decades. In my work, I have encountered phenomenally effective strategies—and also others that were less than effective. And, I have had extensive direct experience in strategy matters in competitive athletics, business management, investing, academic and other involvements. I express my appreciation to those I have encountered through these involvements, from whom I have learned much, some of which learning is presented in this book.

I acknowledge with respect and gratitude those whose best practices examples—as well as numerous "not quite ready for prime time" examples—provide the basis for the lessons that are the foundation of this book. Considerations of space and propriety preclude my mentioning all of these individuals, so I am applying a variant of the disclaimer that the names have been changed and/or omitted, to protect the innocent—and not so innocent.

This book, as with my other writings, has benefited from many ongoing conversations with professional colleagues, clients and others about their strategy matters. Colleagues in Roulac Group who have been with me over the last several decades have stimulated and enhanced my insights into the strategy process. Nancy Fitzpatrick and Michael Hanrahan provided editorial and technical review of the manuscript. Layla Smith designed and typeset this book. Carol Gallivan, Dwight Loop and Kathleen Nosek assisted with manuscript preparation and production. I am very grateful for this help and support, often in the face of daunting pressure and heavy workloads.

I also wish to acknowledge and thank my professional colleagues who reviewed the manuscript and provided helpful comments including: John W. Bickel II, Roger Franz, Thomas J. Frey, William E. Halal, Kirk O. Hanson, Erich A. Helfert, Roger Herman, Arthur B. Laffer, Pam Lontos, Norm Matson, T.J. Rohleder, Brian Tracy and Loren Volk.

The lessons reflected *421 Strategy Mistakes and How You Can Avoid Them* were inevitably learned through long hours preparing for and participating in strategy matters, which work can mandate realigning family schedules. I am most appreciative of my family for their understanding and patience. On more than a few occasions the observations that my son, Arthur, my daughter, Fiona, and my wife, Olivia Denise Parkinson have offered have amplified and illuminated my understanding of the matters in which I was involved and subject matter of the mistakes described in this book in particular.

To all who have contributed and have been associated with this work, I say, thank you and Namasté.

Stephen E. Roulac
January 2004

About the Author

Stephen Roulac is the world's leading authority on the economic productivity and strategic importance of the places in which we live, work, learn, play, shop and prosper. His provocative vision of the future of place strategy and property investing stimulates insights that lead to extraordinary business performance and personal effectiveness. Through his high level private and public advisory relationships, business and investing strategies, seminal writings, and provocative presentations throughout the world, Stephen Roulac is—arguably more than any other individual—advancing the thought processes of leaders who consider the future from both business and academic perspectives.

Stephen Roulac is CEO of Roulac Global Places LLC, the place strategy and real estate advisory firm with offices in the San Francisco area, Hong Kong, and Hyderabad, India. Roulac Global Places achieves extraordinary outcomes for its clients—located in every continent of the world—through integrating insights and understanding of both real estate properties and businesses operating within the real estate industry, the significant impacts of real estate capital markets, plus corporate business strategies. With extensive experience in all property types, debt and equity positions, security forms and specialized property interests, he has qualified and testified as an expert witness in more than 100 complex, high-stakes business and real estate litigation matters.

Stephen Roulac is a recipient of the James A. Graaskamp Award for iconoclastic thinking that advances real estate paradigms and the Warner Bloomberg Award for promoting a vision of the future established on principles of social justice. He was named a

Millennium Real Estate Award Honoree by the U.C. Berkeley Fisher Center for Real Estate and Urban Economics, recognizing those 100 individuals who have had the greatest impact upon the real estate industry in the twentieth century.

Much in demand as a professional speaker, Stephen Roulac is the author of hundreds of articles and books, many of which are considered landmarks. A leading academic and past president of the American Real Estate Society, he holds the position of Professor of Global Property Strategy, School of the Built Environment at University of Ulster, Belfast, Northern Ireland. His credentials include PhD, Stanford; JD, University of California, Berkeley; MBA, Harvard; and BA, Pomona, and he holds the AICP, CMC and CPA professional designations.

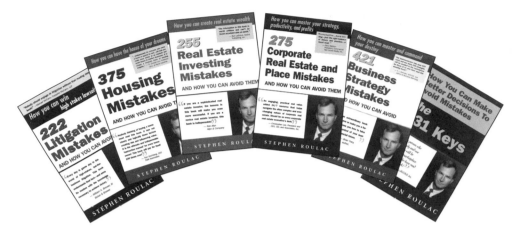

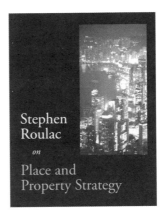

You Can Receive Free Reports

You can receive six informative free reports that tell you more about how to apply the lessons from this book. You can choose from the following reports:

- How You Can Create Your Winning Real Estate Investing Strategy
- Forgotten "P" of Marketing
- How You Can Win High Stakes Litigation
- How Corporate Real Estate and Place Strategies Can Improve Business Profits and Increase Shareholder Wealth
- Everything the Professional Manager Working in a Real Estate Company Wants to Know But Does Not Know To Ask
- What the Administrative Professional Needs to Know about the Real Estate Business

A description of each of these ***free reports*** appears on the following pages.

To order your free report please contact us in any of the following ways:

Email: freereports@roulac.com
Phone: 1-888-765-1895
Fax: 415-451-4343
Mail: Property Press, 709 Fifth Avenue, San Rafael, CA 94901

Please provide your name, mailing address, phone number, and fax. Please specify which free reports you would like to receive.

FREE REPORT 1

How You Can Create Your Winning Real Estate Investing Strategy

More people have made fortunes in real estate than in any other category of economic activity. No entrepreneurial activity offers as much reward with as few barriers to entry as real estate. Real estate literally can be your path to riches.

But real estate is also fraught with peril. Real estate markets tend to be inefficient—meaning that there is simultaneously a high reward for expertise and a big penalty for miscalculation. The downside in real estate is much bigger than it is in much more familiar investments such as the stock market.

Recent significant events suggest that real estate markets may become even more rewarding—and even more risky—than ever before. In this exclusive free report you can learn what you need to know about *How You Can Create Your Winning Real Estate Investing Strategy.*

Please provide your name, mailing address, phone number, and fax and request the *How You Can Create Your Winning Real Estate Investing Strategy* free report.

To order your free report:

Email: freereports@roulac.com
Phone: 1-888-765-1895
Fax: 415-451-4343
Mail: Property Press, 709 Fifth Avenue, San Rafael, CA 94901

Free Report 2

Forgotten "P" of Marketing

Everyone in marketing is taught the importance of *promotion, pricing, product* and *packaging*. But while *place* is also included in marketing education, *place* is essentially the *Forgotten "P" of Marketing.*

Are you an entrepreneur committed to building and expanding your business? Are you a senior executive responsible for your company's destiny? Are you a marketing professional?

If you answer yes to any of these questions, you cannot afford to miss this free report, where you can learn the extraordinary possibilities related to place in marketing.

Why is place important?

- Place defines customer value and satisfaction.
- Place is integral to product positioning.
- Place can be the essence of the offer.
- Place branding can make all the difference.
- Place can be central to defining the value proposition.

Please provide your name, mailing address, phone number, and fax and request the *Forgotten "P" of Marketing* free feport.

To order your free report:

Email: freereports@roulac.com
Phone: 1-888-765-1895
Fax: 415-451-4343
Mail: Property Press, 709 Fifth Avenue, San Rafael, CA 94901

Free Report 3

How You Can Win High-Stakes Litigation

Are you a lawyer whose clients sometimes are involved in high-stakes litigation? Are you a litigator who advocates your clients' interests in high stakes lawsuits? Are you someone who is involved as a party in litigation?

If you answer yes to any of these questions, you cannot afford to miss this powerful free report that tells you what you need to known to prevail in the ultimate intellectual combat—high stakes litigation.

You will learn the mindsets, strategies, preparation, resources, tactics and more that make the difference between victory and defeat in lawsuits that you cannot afford to lose.

If you are a party to high stakes litigation, you cannot afford to miss this free report, *How You Can Win High Stakes Litigation.*

Please provide your name, mailing address, phone number, and fax and request the *How You Can Win High Stakes Litigation* free report.

To order your free report:

Email: freereports@roulac.com
Phone: 1-888-765-1895
Fax: 415-451-4343
Mail: Property Press, 709 Fifth Avenue, San Rafael, CA 94901

Free Report 4

How Corporate Real Estate and Place Strategies Can Improve Business Profits and Increase Shareholder Wealth

Are you a senior executive with responsibility for your company's destiny? Are you an investor who wants to understand how to identify companies that will outperform their competitors? Are you a real estate professional working with corporations concerning their real estate and place invovlements?

If you answer yes to any of these questions, then you need to know the valuable information you can access in the free report, *How Corporate Real Estate and Place Strategies Can Improve Business Profits and Increase Shareholder Wealth.*

Although it is widely recognized that successful corporations are successful by pursuing superior corporate business strategies, less recognized is the important role that a good corporate real estate strategy can play in supporting business success. And less understood is the critical difference that a superior place strategy can make in enabling a company to achieve breakout financial performance relative to its competitors.

If you are a senior corporate executive, a sophisticated investor, or a professional working with business real estate, then you need the information you can gain in this free valuable special report, *How Corporate Real Estate and Place Strategies Can Improve Business Profits and Increase Shareholder Wealth.*

Please provide your name, mailing address, phone number, and fax and request the *How Corporate Real Estate and Place Strategies Can Improve Business Profits and Increase Shareholder Wealth* free report.

Free Report 5

Everything the Professional Manager Working in a Real Estate Company Wants to Know But Does Not Know to Ask

Are you a professional manager working in a real estate company? Are there some important topics in real estate that you want to know about? Do you recognize that knowing more about real estate can enable you to be even more effective, productive and successful in your work?

If you answer yes to any of these questions, then you must get the free special report, *What the Professional Manager Working in a Real Estate Company Wants to Know But Does Not Know to Ask.*

This special report will help you understand how you can apply your professional and managerial knowledge to the workings of companies operating in the real estate business. The knowledge in this special report will be instrumental in your obtaining successful outcomes in your professional work.

Please provide your name, mailing address, phone number, and fax and request the *Everything the Professional Manager Working in a Real Estate Company Wants to Know But Does Not Know to Ask* free report.

Free Report 6

What the Administrative Professional Needs to Know About the Real Estate Business

Do you work in an important administrative professional role in a real estate business? Are you interested in the administrative professional opportunities in real estate businesses? Do you have executive responsibility in a real estate company that employs administrative professionals?

If you answer yes to any of these questions, you cannot afford not to learn *What the Administrative Professional Needs to Know About the Real Estate Business.*

It may be surprising to consider that the majority of people working in the real estate business do not have any background or direct training in real estate. But today, dramatic changes in the real estate business mean that training is ever more important, yet is all too little available in most real estate organizations.

What the Administrative Professional Needs to Know About the Real Estate Business free report tells you what you need to know to get ahead in your career, to get ahead in your company, to get a better job, to do a better job—to be more valuable to yourself and your company.

Please provide your name, mailing address, phone number, and fax and request the *What the Administrative Professional Needs to Know in the Real Estate Business* free report.

To order your free report:

Email: freereports@roulac.com
Phone: 1-888-765-1895
Fax: 415-451-4343
Mail: Property Press, 709 Fifth Avenue, San Rafael, CA 94901